REALITY AND REFORM
IN CLINICAL
TEACHER EDUCATION

REALITY AND REFORM
IN CLINICAL
TEACHER EDUCATION

Edited by
James V. Hoffman
Sara A. Edwards
Assistant Editor
Liz Gold

RANDOM HOUSE   NEW YORK
This book was developed for Random House by Lane Akers, Inc.

First Edition

9 8 7 6 5 4 3 2

The work reported herein was performed pursuant to a grant from the National Institute of Education, Department of Education. However, the opinions expressed
herein do not necessarily reflect the position or policy of the National Institute of
Education, and no official endorsement by the National Institute of Education
should be inferred.

Library of Congress Cataloging-in-Publication Data

Reality and reform in clinical teacher education.

  Bibliography: p.
  1. Student teaching—United States.   2. Teachers—
In-service training—United States.   I. Hoffman,
James V. II. Edwards, Sara.
LB2157.U5R43 1986   370′.7′330973   86-3848
ISBN 0-394-36349-3

Designed and Composed by The Bookmakers, Incorporated, Wilkes-Barre, Pennsylvania

Manufactured in the United States of America

Contents

Foreword:
1000 Leaps Ahead
in Clinical Education

Virginia Richardson Koehler

This volume is concerned with clinical teacher education, believed to be the most useful form of teacher education and staff development but seldom and poorly practiced. Clinical education has its place in preservice teacher education—primarily during student teaching—in beginning teacher programs, and in inservice education.

Student teaching involves structured teaching experiences in the natural setting of the classroom, in combination with positive and corrective feedback from a college supervisor and the cooperating teacher in whose classroom the student is practicing. Summaries of research on preservice teacher education point to the importance of the student teaching experience.[1] Practicing teachers who are asked about the relative importance of their courses in preservice teacher education invariably rate student teaching the highest. It is only later on—starting from their third to fifth year—that they begin to appreciate the academic elements of their preservice preparation.

But preservice students should not be expected to become effective teachers on their first day of teaching. No other professions expect this, and the teaching profession should not either. Furthermore, recent research points to the developmental nature of learning how to teach. Beginning teachers think about their classrooms in very different ways than experienced teachers.[2] Beginning teachers should therefore be receiving the type of help that is an extension of student teaching; that is, they should be working with a clinical professional who is able to observe them teach and provide helpful feedback. Thus, the beginners can be helped through those difficult early years to become truly effective, experienced teachers who have not developed a set of coping mechanisms that are detrimental to learning.

Observation and feedback have been shown to be also important in helping inservice teachers improve. The literature on improving and effective schools points to the importance of norms of collegiality, in which teachers talk to each other about instruction, and observe and provide feedback to each other.[3] In learning how to teach, and learning how to teach better, observation with feedback—in other words, clinical supervision—can be a powerful tool. Unfortunately, clinical supervision, although mentioned often, is seldom used in inservice—including beginning—teaching. And Little points out the paucity of school situations in which the norms of collegiality exist.[4]

While acknowledging the importance of clinical supervision at all stages, one also has to consider the quality of its application. Investigations of clinical feedback during student teaching have found it lacking in substance, criticism, and depth. The RITE study of preservice clinical education found little in clinical feedback sessions that related to the student teachers' formal pedagogical education, or to research on teaching. The feedback was particularistic and provided few explanations.[5]

This volume presents a conceptual framework of clinical education and ways of thinking about its application. It will make an enormous contribution toward improving this extremely important process. Three attributes of the material presented here extend the work on clinical supervision by leaps and bounds. First, it is research-based. This work is based on three major studies which themselves were based on extensive reviews of the research literature (see Appendix A). Second, the framework is generic, and can therefore be applied to preservice, beginning, and inservice programs. And third, and most importantly, this framework incorporates a research-based model of effective teaching. For the last fifteen years, prescriptions for clinical supervision have been process-oriented. That is, they have suggested how a supervisor should approach the meeting with a supervisee—be direct or nondirect, have a goals-oriented or open-ended discussion, etc. But seldom has there been a discussion of the content of clinical conferences. What are the supervisors to look for? What aspects of teaching and learning should be discussed? The framework in this book encompasses current research on effective teaching along with other knowledge bases which, in turn, can become the content of the clinical process.

This volume, then, will allow us to make sense of clinical education and therefore to move forward with a solid research base to improve this most important element of teacher education.

Acknowledgments

The authors wish to express their gratitude to the National Institute of Education and in particular to Joe Vaughan for his support and encouragement in the preparation of this book. Also, a special thanks to Freddie Green who has served the RITE research effort faithfully as administrative assistant throughout its history. Her attention to the multitude of details associated with the symposia that formed the basis for this book and her diligent working through of the many drafts of this manuscript are much appreciated.

Introduction

The Research in Teacher Education (RITE) program of the Research and Development Center for Teacher Education at The University of Texas at Austin was formed in the fall of 1980 under the direction of Gary A. Griffin. Plans were laid at that time for a comprehensive investigation of the clinical component of teacher education programs at preservice, induction, and in-service levels. In the years that followed, RITE researchers conducted a series of three major studies. The first was a multi-site, multi-method investigation of the preservice clinical teacher education experience commonly referred to as student teaching. The purpose was to describe the people, practices, and outcomes of the student teaching experience, with attention given to the characteristics of the participants, their interactions, and the nature of the contexts within which student teaching takes place. The second effort was a quasi-experimental inquiry into the effects of leadership training for staff development personnel on teacher effectiveness and development. The focus of this study was clinical teacher education at the inservice level. The third study was an effort to describe how certain state-mandated teacher induction programs affected the transition from student of teaching to teacher. (See Appendix A for brief descriptions of the three studies.)

As the third study approached completion, the RITE staff began to turn their attention to the task of integrating the findings from these three studies in terms of implications for effective clinical practices. A number of strategies were employed to achieve this end. First, members of the RITE research staff conducted secondary analyses of the data from the studies with the goal of uncovering patterns of effective clinical practice. The aggregate data base for the three studies is extensive. Participants in the studies included 93 student teachers, 125 experienced classroom teachers, 25 university personnel, 16 first-year teachers, and 24 administrators/staff developers. There were 494 interviews conducted and transcribed, 3,367 journal entries collected and reviewed, and 557 classroom observations made and summarized. In addition, data were collected on many of the participants using a variety of tests, questionnaires, and inventories.

The second strategy was to engage the services of a group of consultants to assist the RITE staff in the task of integrating these findings across studies. Four outstanding researchers in teacher education worked with the project for over a year assisting in the analysis and interpretation of the RITE data. The consultants were Hilda Borko, Willis Copeland, Beatrice Ward, and Kenneth Zeichner. They brought to the project not only their individual expertise in the area of clinical teacher education, but also fresh perspectives on the research that had been conducted.

The third strategy was to convene a series of three one-day colloquia on the topic of effective practices in clinical teacher education. The first colloquium was held on the campus of the University of California at Santa Barbara and focused on clinical practices at the inservice level. The second was held in Falls Church, Virginia, and hosted by Virginia Tech University. It focused on clinical practices at the induction level. The third was held at the University of Illinois at Chicago and focused on the preservice level. The RITE staff and the consultants attended each of these colloquia. The key participants were local experts in clinical teacher education who were invited to discuss the RITE findings (see Appendix B). During these sessions, a theoretical framework for clinical teacher education derived from the RITE research was presented and discussed. Participants in the colloquia offered their responses and suggestions. As a result of these interactions, the framework was revised and extended. These sessions also provided an opportunity to examine carefully the implications of this framework for effective teacher education practices at the preservice, induction, and inservice levels.

What evolved from this year-long process was, first and foremost, an integrated RITE proposal for effective clinical teacher education, with its implications for reform in practice. This framework and its implications are the primary focus of this book. However, in the process, the RITE framework outgrew its original "authorship" or "ownership." What started as a localized RITE research team effort became a collective effort of all those who contributed their ideas and vision, especially the consultants and the experts who participated in the colloquia. Though the individual chapters in this book carry author identification, the reader will often find use of such terms as "we" and "the RITE group" in reference to the clinical teacher education framework. This language correctly reflects the source of the framework and the degree of advocacy taken by each of the authors represented in this book.

JAMES V. HOFFMAN
SARA A. EDWARDS

Clinical Teacher Education

Gary A. Griffin

What is good teaching? Who is the effective teacher? These questions occupy the thoughts of professional educators, researchers, and, it is safe to say, a large segment of the general public. Professional educators, whether in a school system or a college or university, answer the questions explicitly and implicitly as they select candidates for teacher education programs, provide learning opportunities for preservice students, appoint teachers to schools and classrooms, provide professional development opportunities, evaluate teachers, and accept or reject teacher candidates for certification and licensure. All of these activities are, in some manner, guided by a conception of what is "good" in teaching and in teachers.

Some of the conceptions of "good" are rooted in recent research on teaching (e.g., a good teacher appropriately delivers direct instruction),[1] others in propositions about teaching derived from philosophical stances (e.g., a good teacher empowers students to attain the ideal of "the good life"),[2] still others in beliefs about the importance of interpersonal relationships (e.g., a good teacher has consistently positive rapport with students),[3] and still others in a set of expectations about the impact of schooling on the larger society (e.g., a good teacher believes that schools can and should "dare to change the social order").[4] Each of these conceptions of the ideal teacher rests upon assumptions about effectiveness, assumptions that guide professional education, evaluation, certification, tenure, and more recently, the award of "mastery" status.

Central to any consideration of the effective or good teacher is the set of decisions about how to foster effectiveness, decisions that guide teacher education programs at preservice, induction, and inservice levels of implementation. Teacher education is typically conceived of as collegiate preservice programs, but there is a growing consensus that this view is too limiting when we think of teachers as professionals who learn, grow, and change throughout their careers.[5] Although the divisions are still somewhat arbitrary, both conceptually and practically, an appealing view of teacher education is that it formally begins in preservice programs in colleges and universities, continues during the first years of teaching in elementary and secondary schools, and extends through time until that point when the teacher elects to leave teaching.

Whether considered segmentally or as a comprehensive program of opportunities to learn and grow, in teacher education a number of influences are brought to bear upon the development of teaching effectiveness. Although there are those who believe that teaching is the consequence of certain innate human properties ("You either can teach or you can't"), most scholars and practitioners would agree that, at the very least, teachers must have command of a body of knowledge and skill in order to be consistently effective.[6] That body of knowledge and skill is presented to teacher candidates and teacher professionals in a number of forms, singly and in interaction. (It has been claimed, on the other hand, that teachers teach as they were taught and that formal teacher education programs have little impact upon altering, modestly or radically, that powerful influence.[7] This conclusion, if true, probably rests upon the inadequacy of particular teacher education programs of study.)

Teacher educators and educational researchers, however, are increasingly emphasizing the power of systematic programs of teacher education to cause teaching to occur in certain well-defined ways.[8] This emphasis is largely the result of the growing number of studies of the consequences of teacher education programs. Although there is not clear-cut evidence that certain programs are more effective in causing "good" teaching than others, and there may never be such evidence due to the complexity of the enterprise, it is possible to claim that teachers are more effective as a result of some intentional teacher education activity than when they enter teaching without such preparation.

Teacher education, of course, is a complicated amalgam of program components and personal/professional variables. Because most believe that teachers should be broadly knowledgeable about central cultural ideas and disciplines, general education is usually part of a teacher education program. Those who believe that teachers are powerful influences upon the development and refinement of students' systems of values draw attention to teacher education program features that help to clarify teachers' own positions about the individual in the society and the role of education in empowering students. And, importantly, based on the central tenet that teaching is professional activity that is influenced and guided by what can be called professional studies, most programs include opportunities to learn about, and how to do, the work of teaching.

One element of teacher education programs where many of the essential variables come together is what has come to be called *clinical teacher education*. Clinical teacher education is the set of learning opportunities that take place in ongoing "real world" classrooms and schools. There is strong evidence that it is from these experiences in these places that prospective teachers and career teachers increase knowledge of their craft, come to depend upon some professional practices rather than others, derive their satisfaction and encounter their disappointments, and either grow toward effectiveness or resign themselves to conducting business as usual: that is, where some teachers burn out while others grow in knowledge, skill, and enthusiasm.[9]

It is this component, clinical teacher education, that is the focus of this chapter and of this book. The proposals here have grown out of a program of research studies that began in 1980. It was then that the Research in Teacher Education (RITE) program was created at the Research and Development Center for Teacher Education at The University of Texas at Austin. In the years from 1980 to 1985, the RITE research team conducted a set of studies with the express intention of better understanding the nature and effects of clinical teacher education in the United States. The studies included three major efforts:

1. a comprehensive multi-method, multi-site descriptive study of student teaching (clinical teacher education as a function of cooperative relationships between universities and elementary and secondary schools);[10]
2. an experimental study of inservice teacher education and leadership (clinical teacher education as a function of the relationship between instructional leaders and teachers);[11] and
3. an analytic study of formal state-mandated teacher induction programs (clinical teacher education connected by state law and regulation to the certification and licensure of beginning teachers).[12]

Although the three major studies differed in features, they were all concerned with contributing to understanding how clinical teacher education is carried forward, how participants and outsiders describe it, the influence of context on the educational opportunities, and the effects of the programs both on the participants and on the contexts where they were brought to life. The three studies, then, despite differences in intentions and participants, can be looked at in terms of common features of clinical teacher education that appear to be strongly related to positive outcomes.

During the period of the RITE studies, researchers in other parts of the United States were also engaged in studying teacher education programs. These studies often included the clinical components of teacher education programs and, therefore, can be used to supplement and complement the generalizations drawn from the RITE work. In some instances, these studies were not conceptualized as inquiries into teacher education, but their research questions, methodologies, and conceptualizations make them natural companions to the RITE efforts.[13] (The effective schools studies, for instance, consistently attend to school variables that contribute to teacher growth and change.)

The discussion of clinical teacher education in these pages is not meant to suggest that learning about and how to do teaching occurs *only* in clinical settings. We believe strongly that clinical education is but one aspect of a broader conception of teacher education. For preservice teachers, this more comprehensive program would include a strong general education component and systematic exposure to and testing of modes of instruction, curriculum planning models, and other professional concepts. For career teachers, clinical education should be embedded in a complex plan of professional growth that includes self-study, participation in advanced graduate degree programs, involvement with professional associations, and the like. (See Chapter 6 for an extended view of a comprehensive teacher education program.) The clinical aspect of a teacher's growth into professional status, then, is considered necessary but insufficient. It is just a part, albeit an important and central part, of a comprehensive program of study and practice.

The features of clinical teacher education programs presented in the remainder of this chapter have been found to be consistently related to positive outcomes, according both to the perceptions of participants in the programs and to expert judgments. It is believed that these features are critical in the planning and conducting of clinical teacher education, whether for preservice students, beginning teachers, or career professionals. Other chapters in the volume will suggest the usefulness of the conceptualization of clinical teacher education presented here for thinking about and improving clinical teacher education programs in the future.

THE IDEAL TEACHER

This chapter began with two questions: What is good teaching? Who is the effective teacher? In order to suggest appropriate and meaningful teacher education programs, we must come to grips with answering those complex questions.[14]

Many propositions about what good teaching is can be found in professional literature, newspaper articles, community talk, and individual perspectives. Because in this chapter we suggest certain critical features of teacher education programs, it is necessary to elaborate on the conception of a "good" teacher that guided the selection of those features. With this conception in mind, the reader can see the relationships between the characteristics of the ideal teacher and the features of the teacher education program.

There are probably as many views about teachers as there are people who have come in contact with them. Typical conceptions range from the strict but kindly teacher (remember Miss Dove?) through the bumbling but eventually effective academician (Mr. Chips?) to the slightly acerbic and mishap-prone post-teenager (Miss Brooks?). In all likelihood, reactions to these and other stereotypes will be shaped and modified by one's world view, notions about the role of the school in the society, ideas about the past and the future, convictions regarding the nature of learning groups, and so on. What follows is a set of teacher characteristics that we value and that have strong support from experts on teaching.

The good teacher is a classroom leader and an authority figure. In this role, the teacher is well-organized, alert to classroom events, concerned about classroom groups as well as about individuals, and skillful in the management of a complex social system. This management takes the form of both exercise of "teacher authority" and delegation of decision-making to students. Furthermore, the management is rooted in a set of beliefs about designated leadership and emergent leadership. The class members' views are solicited and actively listened to. There are opportunities for students to work independently and in both small and large groups. The classroom environment can be characterized as orderly, friendly, attractive, and, with occasional planned exceptions, academically purposeful.

The teacher contributes to this environment through the ability to diagnose cognitive and social behaviors of students, act upon the diagnoses in meaningful and informed ways, and reflect upon the apparent effects of his or her actions. The teacher monitors the understandings of the students systematically and continually. This monitoring is obvious to students and observers alike. The teacher is able to monitor learning as well as more obvious behavior through advanced planning and continuous evaluation. Furthermore, the teacher uses information collected during monitoring to make instructional decisions as well as judgments about student progress.

The ideal teacher is in command of subject matter and is also aware of a set of options for delivering that subject matter so that effective, efficient, and long-term learning takes place. When it is necessary to move beyond what is already known, the teacher engages in self-study of both the content and the nature of his or her instruction. The self-study is a part of sense-making, a central aspect of being a teacher, and is transmitted by example as a valued enterprise to students.

The teacher interacts with others in the school, recognizing that the school's members have shared problems, and works with others on issues of particular concern to the school. Soliciting advice and seeking counsel from colleagues, teachers, and administrators, the teacher seeks out opportunities to "have a voice" in school matters, to be an authority with a forum.

The teacher understands the importance of the home-school relationship and acts upon that understanding by formulating, coordinating, and participating in opportunities to become a positive force in the lives of individual students and the school as a whole. The teacher cooperates with parents in the enormously important tasks associated with educating a citizenry, facing controversy not quixotically but rationally and with convictions based upon a well-developed set of values that can be articulated readily. And the teacher understands the difficulties related to providing educational opportunities to an increasingly heterogeneous population.

The ideal teacher is aware of the central but often maligned role of the teacher in the problem-laden social institution of the school. This awareness, instead of leading to a sense of defeatism or, perhaps worse, resigned indifference, leads to a commitment to re-create that institution. In doing this, the teacher participates with others in problem-solving, developing and testing alternatives, sharing successes and failures with colleagues, and adopting and adapting solutions to persistent dilemmas. In this process, the individual is a central decision-maker, aware of the complex nature of schooling, capable of adjusting ideas and behavior when evidence suggests the need, and able to see situations from multiple perspectives even when those perspectives are contrary to the teacher's own.

In going about the work of teaching, this ideal teacher is guided by a set of carefully formulated values, beliefs, information, and skills. The teacher is a learner, a person whose professional education does not end upon receipt of an undergraduate or graduate degree and a certificate to teach. The teacher learns through experience and reflection, participating in professional organizations, electing to be a part of formal educative programs, and staying informed about advances in teaching and schooling through independent initiative. These activities lead the teacher toward what can be termed a "risk-taking" stance, a professional disposition toward trying out new ideas, implementing new practices, and thinking about teaching in different ways. The risks, however, are reasoned choices for professional engagement. They are not capricious or faddish.

In summary, the ideal teacher is a knowledgeable, well-organized, and consistent classroom leader who interacts with students, colleagues, and patrons purposefully and effectively. This individual sees teaching as more than meeting with students, and works with peers on identifying and acting on problems at classroom and school levels of the system. The teacher values this opportunity to be an integral school decision-maker, and others value the teacher's perceptions and knowledge of desirable practice.

Of course, it is highly unlikely that the clinical teacher education framework that is proposed here can, by itself, contribute to the development of this paragon of teaching excellence. The RITE research team and others concerned with teacher education, however, are convinced that programs that match the model are more likely to lead teachers to think and behave in these ways than programs that markedly differ from it.

Furthermore, we believe that the critical features of the framework must all be in place for the program to have the desired influence. Just as certain effects are more intense when chemicals are combined than when administered singly, the effectiveness of the RITE clinical teacher education framework will be greatest, we believe, when all the program features interact.

It must be kept in mind that the RITE framework is focused on only the clinical aspects of teacher education. For maximum power, this clinical component must be buttressed by soundly formulated and implemented programs of general education; engaged in by those who have personal propensities for providing quality instruction; preceded, accompanied, and followed by professional studies rooted in the most reliable knowledge available; and delivered by teacher educators, staff developers, and principals whose professional interactions are at the highest level of practice.

THE RITE CLINICAL TEACHER EDUCATION FRAMEWORK

The research and theory we have identified suggest one defining property and seven critical features of an effective clinical teacher education program, whether that program is at preservice, induction, or inservice levels of implementation. The program must be *embedded in a school context* (defining property), and be (1) *context-sensitive,* (2) *purposeful and articulated,* (3) *participatory and collaborative,* (4) *knowledge-based,* (5) *ongoing,* (6) *developmental, and* (7) *analytic and reflective.* There is an obvious conceptual difference between the defining property and the critical features. The defining property sets the boundaries within which the RITE framework of clinical teacher education is to be envisioned, implemented, and monitored. The critical features are the program characteristics that must be present *within* the defining property. The defining property and each of the critical features are presented in turn, although the effectiveness of the RITE framework is dependent upon the interaction of *all* of the features over time.

Defining property: The program is defined by its relations with a school context. The hallmark of a clinical teacher education program is its relation to the context in which it is carried forward. In contrast to general education and professional studies — typical components of teacher education — clinical teacher education takes place in living classrooms and schools. These real-life contexts and the people in them give form and substance to clinical teacher education. It is commonly believed that learning *about* teaching and schooling in colleges and universities differs sharply from learning to *do* teaching and schooling in elementary and secondary schools.

Currently, two views of the relation of context to the preparation and continuing growth of teachers prevail. One view holds that nothing of real importance is learned until a person is faced with the daily problems and possibilities posed by students in classrooms. This idea is often expressed as the dichotomy between the "ivory tower" of the university and the "real life" of schools. (It is unfortunate that the real-life image also is often put forward in combative terms such as "the trenches" or "the battlefields.") According to those holding this view, the university deals with theory whereas the schools teach the more practical and more highly valued skills necessary to become effective as a teacher. Indeed, there are teacher education programs currently in operation that depend solely upon successful practice in schools for determination of teacher adequacy, even for the purpose of granting state certification.[15]

There is another, more comprehensive view of the role of context in the education of teachers.[16] This view acknowledges that the person learns from the context but also gives attention to learning and acting beyond mere *accommodation* to the context.[17] The teacher-context relationship is seen as a means by which the teacher learns about, from, in, and how to act upon the context. Rather than learning only how schools operate at a technological level, the teacher candidate or beginning teacher learns why the classrooms and schools look the way they do, what conditions constrain or promote teaching and learning activity, how schools come to develop their often very special characters, how to subject schools to disciplined inquiry and analysis, and, importantly, how to act upon school and classroom contexts for the purpose of improvement.

Clearly, in the first of these two views, teacher education is divorced from context and can have only limited import because it is "theory without practice." In the second, however, we see the potential for teacher education to provide essential theoretical foundations applied in such a way that practice will be better understood and subject to change *and* improvement.

Feature #1: The program is context-sensitive. Currently, teachers and other school personnel are expressing considerable concern about "conditions of work." This is another way of acknowledging the power of context to reward or discourage teachers. Many see unfavorable conditions of work as the primary reasons why some of the finest teachers leave teaching and some of the most promising young people choose not to enter the teaching force. Among the most detrimental conditions is the powerlessness felt by many teachers. They note that their professional authority is often questioned and thereby diminished, and they conclude that they are mere cogs in a wheel whose direction is beyond their control.[18]

A program of clinical teacher education, according to the RITE data and based on the conclusions of other studies, can be especially effective in providing a teacher with the knowledge and skills necessary to become a powerful influence for change in a school, not a person who just accepts contexts and learns to live within sometimes narrowly-conceived intellectual and practical boundaries, but a person who can analyze the realities of a classroom and a school with the goal of making powerful changes for the better.[19] Thus, the teacher-context relationship suggested here is directed toward the teacher's understanding and acting upon situations in which teaching and learning occur.

What this position implies, of course, is that the classrooms and schools of the nation are rich in information directly related to doing teaching and schooling. Furthermore, that information can be used in vitally important ways to prepare people to become teachers and to help new and career teachers grow and develop. Therefore, the context feature of the RITE clinical teacher education framework raises to a central position the characteristics, regularities, relationships, behaviors, and effects of what happens in schools.

Sensitivity to context can be accomplished in a number of ways. Prospective teachers, for example, are typically required to spend time in classrooms. How that time is spent, however, will determine whether or not the context is central to the teacher candidate's movement toward professional status. A field experience that is unfocused, lacking in concurrent expert guidance, and unconnected to developing ways of seeing and understanding the classroom context would clearly not meet the standard set forth here.[20] Similarly, opportunities for new and career teachers to become expert in teaching that either ignore the contexts in which teaching is to take place or that only sporadically give attention to the situation-specific nature of teaching would also fall outside the RITE framework's specifications.

Clearly, there are dramatic qualitative differences between school contexts. Some are harsh and punishing whereas others are inviting and rewarding. A context that is to be a central stimulus for positive teacher growth must nurture rather than blunt that growth. A nurturing context would, for example, have as norms strong and positive leadership, a high degree of professional collegiality, clear and public expectations for adult and student behavior, and a well-developed sense of mission.

There is currently talk of teacher "warranties." These guarantees generally promise that a teacher graduate will be a successful teacher; if not, the teacher education institution will "fix" the teacher through campus or school-based reeducation. Although this notion has some appeal, it founders on a lack of understanding of how *where* a teacher teaches affects *how* a teacher teaches. Just as an automobile manufacturer's warranty does not apply to a driver who abuses his or her car, teaching effectiveness cannot be guaranteed in school contexts that abuse teachers and prospective teachers.

Contexts as discussed in this volume, then, are assumed to be positive environments for learning the important social and professional manifestations of teaching. It is in these exemplary settings that clinical teacher education should take place. However, contexts in the organizational forms of schools and classrooms become not just the places where one learns the conventions of these places as they are, but also sources of information for understanding teaching and schooling, and opportunities for analysis and attempts at improvement.

It will be clear to the reader that the other program features of clinical teacher education are ones that could be present in any component of a teacher education program, not just the clinical component. These features would contribute, for example, to the strength of a program in professional studies that is college-based, as well as to planned professional education opportunities provided for members of teacher organizations. For clinical teacher education, however, the six features are enhanced and strengthened in direct relation to the degree to which they are responsive to and influential upon teachers in school and classroom contexts.

Feature #2: The program is purposeful and articulated. It is conventional wisdom that schools are instruments of social intention. Yet scholars have noted that the goals of education as seen in schools often overlap and conflict, and that these goals are themselves often ambiguous in nature.[21] That is, although schools are designed by the culture to do something having to do with the education of children and youth, that something is not as clearly defined and articulated as might be expected.

Likewise, the education of teachers at preservice, induction, and inservice levels of activity is often lacking in clear purposes, and the rationales for such programs are seldom well articulated.[22] (Articulation here means the degree of clarity of presentation of ideas. Another meaning related to relationships between parts of a whole is suggested in the section describing the developmental feature of the RITE framework.)

Research conducted by the RITE team and by other scholars strongly demonstrates the positive effects of clear, public expressions of purpose in teacher education programs. Their importance seems close to axiomatic. Unfortunately, negative examples abound. Consider the confusion that occurs when student teachers, cooperating teachers, and university supervisors cannot recall, let alone agree upon, the purposes of their clinical experiences together. Most practicing teachers can tell anecdotes about so-called "inservice days" that appear to have been disconnected events leading to no widely understood purpose. And orientations for new teachers are often devoted to so-called administrivia and unconnected to a comprehensive plan to help teachers in the induction phase of development move successfully into teaching roles.

More positively, research and less formal observation of practice illustrate that some teacher education programs are characterized by conscious and public attention to clarity of purposes.[23] Furthermore, the greater and more widespread the understanding of the purposes, the more likely that they will be realized. After all, if participants in programs are aware of what is expected to be accomplished, it is more probable that the purposes will be met. Clear, specific statements of purpose provide participants with a sense of direction, an expectation that something will be accomplished. Participants who are not informed of well-formulated purposes are placed in the position of trying to second-guess (or outsmart) those responsible for teacher education programs.[24]

It should be understood that the attention to purpose is not put forth as yet another means to coerce prospective or practicing teachers into a conforming stance. Although one purpose of a teacher education program might be as narrow as "to plan lessons according to the sequence of objective, development, motivation, practice, seatwork, and evaluation," another purpose might be as broad as "to identify a school problem, develop a means to act upon it, and teach others in the school ways to use the solution."[25] In either case, highly prescriptive or broadly conceptualized, such statements offer teacher education participants a sense of what is expected, what is valued, what will be supported.

It has been asserted that the purposes of a teacher education program, in addition to being clearly presented, should be "public." What is meant here is that all persons affected by the program should be aware of the purposes and be able to recognize their relationships to program activities. There is evidence that participants in all roles associated with complex teacher education efforts are often unaware of the anticipated outcomes of the programs.[26] It is not uncommon for researchers to receive blank stares or garbled mumblings when they ask, "What is this program expected to accomplish?" On the other hand, two dramatic examples of the power of clearly articulated purposes can be found in the RITE studies. In one, staff developers were given the opportunity to learn which of the teaching behaviors in teacher effectiveness studies were consistently related to positive student outcomes, and then were asked to develop a school-specific plan in which they could include opportunities for teachers to learn about these research findings.[27] The purpose of this effort was for the staff developers to use, *when appropriate*, the research findings in their inservice meetings with teachers. Not only did the staff developers use the findings, but they did it in situationally appropriate ways. That is, they did not engulf their teacher colleagues with all they had learned; they "mixed and matched" according to their understanding of a school and the teachers in it. This illustration shows that a broad conception of purpose can lead toward desired ends, in this case the introduction of research-based propositions about effective teaching. (This is in sharp contrast to programs that require all teachers to use in the same ways an entire set of prescriptions for practice.)

The other example emerges from a study of new teacher programs. In one of the programs the purposes were stated clearly and explicitly in terms of what beginning teachers were expected to demonstrate in order to be granted state certification. Although one might question the wisdom of applying such expectations across the entire group of teachers located in very different schools and classrooms, it was evident that the explicit nature of the expectations and the clarity and public nature of their presentation to beginning teachers were related to the high degree of demonstration of the teaching behaviors among the group of new teachers.[28]

In sum, then, the RITE clinical teacher education framework requires that teacher education programs have explicit purposes, whether they be specific or general, and that these purposes be clearly articulated and widely understood.

Feature #3: The program is participatory and collaborative. Clinical teacher education, as suggested in the discussion of context, is largely a set of interactions between classrooms and schools and the people in them. These interactions are believed to be most effective when characterized by participation and collaboration.[29]

Participation, of course, can mean simple responsiveness, in much the same way that animals respond when they hear certain human vocalizations or commands. In the RITE framework, however, we believe participation is of particularly high value when it is well beyond the level of simple response. Participation here refers to active involvement, the give-and-take that characterizes the liveliest professional and intellectual discourse.[30] Participation means active questioning, diligence in the search for reasonable solutions to unreasonable problems, persistence in discovering the most powerful resources for instruction, formulation of important problems for public attention, and so on.

Some researchers call this brand of participation *professional collegiality*.[31] (This is in contrast, but not contradiction, to personal or social collegiality.) The assumption is that teachers, like other professionals, are more effective, and more knowledgeable about that effectiveness, when they have regular opportunities to be actively involved in the advancement of their important work.

Collaboration is an oft-used and ill-understood term, particularly in relation to matters of teaching and schooling. Too often, collaboration is a label applied to what can at best be called co-optation, the act of convincing teachers that they are true partners when, in fact, they are unwittingly doing another's bidding. There are few true examples of collaboration in educational settings, whether they be students in classroom groups or teachers and administrators working together in the same school.

Collaboration, however, is central to the RITE framework of clinical teacher education because of its power for strengthening a professional development effort, particularly for career teachers, as well as for increasing the *professional dignity* of the participants.[32] Collaboration is related to ownership. The teacher who has had some hand in formulating and carrying forward the effort (as opposed to being only the recipient of a set of externally-imposed specifications) will very probably feel a strong investment in bringing it to successful operation. Also, and perhaps more importantly, teacher education programs for new and experienced teachers are aptly concerned with giving participants more authority in their teaching roles.

Although the role of the "expert" is not to be downgraded, isn't it reasonable to assume that teachers, as they grow in knowledge and experience, will have greater insights into the issues that need to be dealt with than those who are not teachers? Many believe that it has been too long since teachers had a significant hand in the determination of their own professional destinies.[33]

The increasing emphasis upon teachers as recipients of prescriptions for practice, "users" of routinized curricula, and objects of mandates made at state and local levels of policy has significantly eroded the teacher's professional dignity in the eyes of the public and, in fact, in the teachers' views of themselves. There appears to be a deficit model of professional development at work, a set of blanket generalizations about teacher skill and competence that leads to increased emphasis upon correcting unforgivable deficiencies. This mind-set has led, in many instances, to the paraprofessionalization of teaching, wherein teaching is considered a technical (rather than intellectual or substantive) activity, one that is easily taught, efficiently observed, and readily remedied.[34]

The depiction of schools and teaching in this worst-case scenario detracts from efforts to attract strong teacher candidates, hold promising new teachers, and gain professional commitment from career teachers. The RITE framework of clinical teacher education includes the collaborative feature because of the demonstrated power of true collaboration to increase the possibility that teachers will view themselves as professionals, people with specialized knowledge and skill who serve important social ends. Collaboration, when it is authentic, ensures that teachers have individual and collective voices when important decisions are made and when those decisions are enacted in school and classroom practice. Collaboration places teachers in positions of status with administrators and policy-making colleagues such that their ideas and insights become part of the decision structure. Collaboration provides teachers with all-too-often-missing communication lines with others concerned about the quality of educational opportunity. These are the conditions that lead to a conception of professional dignity as a vital component of one's work and one's role in the larger culture.

Feature #4: The program is knowledge-based. As for several of the other features of the RITE framework of clinical teacher education, the specification of a knowledge base to guide practice seems either simplistic or superfluous. Unfortunately, neither conclusion is warranted. A number of teacher education programs appear to be informed more by opinions or impressions than by verified and reliable knowledge.[35] This may be related to the problem often observed by the research community: namely, that teachers in large numbers are relatively unable to speak coherently about why they do what they do in classrooms. Instead of referring to common knowledge about best practice, many teachers can talk only about what they have tried and what has happened as a consequence of those trials.[36] This, of course, is a form of knowledge, but it does not serve as a distinguishing mark of the teacher as professional. It is entirely possible that the lack of attention to the development and distribution of knowledge about teaching and schooling contributes significantly to teachers' observed unfamiliarity with known theory and practice.

We must assert here that knowledge can take many forms and can be derived from a variety of different perspectives. This assertion is particularly necessary when, as in this case, the model being proposed is the product of a research institution that has engaged almost solely in empirical research. The temptation for the reader is to suspect that the term "knowledge" as used here includes only that which can be verified by evidence (or, more particularly, evidence in the form of quantification). However, the term also refers to knowledge that is theoretical, propositional, and rooted in or substantiated by value and craft.[37]

Knowledge here means more than a set of discrete facts, lists, prescriptions, "findings." Knowledge here means a coherent set of such facts and other information that together allow us to make judgments, come to informed decisions, suggest desirable practices, and ask important questions. This knowledge is codified, is connected in its particulars, and is the resting place of concepts and constructs that make sense.

Certainly, recent attention to a rational, empirical view of teaching and schooling has contributed enormously to our understanding of processes and outcomes and the relationships between and among them.[38] The effort of the past fifteen years devoted to understanding what teaching behaviors are associated with what student achievements is of inestimable value to teacher education programs. But total reliance upon this body of knowledge to make major programmatic decisions about teaching, schooling, and teacher education is probably insufficient for the development of the kind of ideal teacher presented earlier in this chapter. In fact, there is some evidence that single-minded dependence upon the process-product teacher effectiveness studies leads to a narrower vision of teaching and teachers than is desired by most professional educators.[39]

In the RITE framework of clinical teacher education, *theoretical knowledge* is of major importance. We agree with the proposition that "theory without practice is futile and practice without theory is fatal," that theory is developed out of practical understanding, and in turn, theory informs practical situations. Theory is particularly powerful in helping prospective and career teachers understand and make sense of their professional worlds. Theoretical formulations suggest and define connections between disparate pieces of the complex teaching and schooling puzzle, and thus lead thoughtful teachers to make their own discoveries as a consequence of increased understandings. They can also provide a body of shared understanding across groups of teachers who are trying to come to decisions about how to proceed in teaching.

A difficulty with using "theory" as a term related to teacher education in general, and to the clinical component of teacher education in particular, is that the word and what it represents have been demeaned over the years by casual and misinformed use. Theory has come to mean for many teachers all of that "stuff" that colleges and universities teach and that teachers can see no meaning for in their practical worlds.[40] What has happened, then, is that the word has come to stand for a good deal of nonsense that passes under the guise of teacher education. Theory, in its very real sense, can be most practical, most useful, and of enormous value to teachers and others in schools. The RITE framework of clinical teacher education recognizes the diminution of the term, but at the same time promotes the recognition of true theoretical formulations as important knowledge for teacher education programs.

The issues that must be dealt with by teachers and others in schools are complex, highly interactive, often imbued with urgency, and increasingly related to societal pressures and influences. Typical responses to this complexity are founded in what can be termed *propositional knowledge*. Propositional knowledge here refers to those ideas for schooling activity that are put forth as proposals, suggestions for change that have yet to be given theoretical or empirical tests of effectiveness. Certainly, the 1960s and 1970s were periods when propositional knowledge in the forms of new curricula, new ways of organizing for instruction, and alternative conceptions of teaching activity were advanced by educational scholars, for the most part, and introduced into schools. It is important in this discussion to stress that propositional knowledge is appropriate for the RITE framework in direct relation to its *promise* for making desirable changes in educational settings. Relative promise rests on the credibility of the person or persons making the proposal, the logical "fit" with the most highly-regarded purposes and practices of schooling, and the degree of comprehensive endorsement from these experts on teaching and schooling. Propositional knowledge, when it meets these implicit criteria, can be an important knowledge base for planning and implementing clinical teacher education programs.

Another conception of knowledge is what has come to be called *craft knowledge*.[41] This body of information, coherent and connected and conceptually whole, emerges out of disciplined practical situations and is cumulative over time. Teachers, individually and collectively, discover that certain practices, certain ways of meeting with students, and certain materials of instruction "work" again and again. This cumulative evidence is, of course, empirical in nature, but it does not have the scientific solidity of the disciplined inquiries discussed earlier in this chapter. It is, in a large sense, a way of viewing the worlds of teaching and schooling from the vantage point of the practitioner who desires above all else that children and youth in schools learn. And when there is evidence that some stimuli for learning are more powerful than others for inducing that learning, another piece of craft wisdom is accumulated.

This craft knowledge is, in fact, the real source of the research findings that emerged from the process-product studies cited earlier. Researchers did not invent the teaching behaviors that were associated with pupil achievement; teachers did. Researchers only discovered that the teaching patterns — craft knowledge in use — were present in the repertoires of teachers whose students scored well on standardized tests. This is not to demean the contribution of the research community. The discoveries are important ones. But it is also important to remember that *teachers*, working out of their own conceptions of craft, were the true inventors, the fundamental improvers, the demonstrators of teaching effectiveness.

Suffice it to say that knowledge can take a variety of forms and can serve a number of functions in learning about teaching, learning how to do teaching, and coming to be a meritorious teacher over a career. The essential point to be made is that the RITE framework demands a reliance upon knowledge in the formulation and implementation of clinical teacher education programs. A program may provide suggestions for teachers to alter their pedagogy; a program may offer knowledge in a form useful for making decisions; a program might even cause teachers to think about what *isn't* known with any certainty and, thereby, promote inquiry. In any case, the attention to knowledge related to the expectations of a clinical program is in direct opposition to the oft-experienced "sink-or-swim" approach to attaining high achievement in teaching.

Feature #5: The program is ongoing. The position taken by the RITE team, and shared by a number of scholars and practitioners, is that teacher education is a continuum, a stream of activity that begins when a person decides to begin professional and academic study leading toward a teaching career, and ends only when the decision is made to end that career. For purposes of convenience as well as demonstrated usefulness, this continuum has been described as having at least three stages: preservice teacher education, induction, and inservice teacher education.[42] (These stages are treated in more detail in Chapters 2, 3, and 4 of this book.)

This conception of teaching suggests that ten years' experience is equal to more than one year taught ten times. It argues against the sameness of teaching activity. It promotes the notion that teachers grow and change, adapt and reconstruct their worlds, and accumulate and discard ideas and practices. When one views teaching activity over time, one is forced to consider that opportunities to learn more and to use that knowledge ever more effectively must somehow be related to one another. In short, teacher education and its clinical component must be ongoing, systematic, and adapted to the stages of the person's growth toward the status of career teacher.[43]

Currently, there are few conceptions of teacher education that take this proposition seriously enough to warrant inclusion in this volume. There is, however, evidence to suggest that clinical teacher education *within stages* ought to be an ongoing activity, rather than the fits and starts that characterize so many efforts in the field. It is not uncommon for the elements of a preservice teacher education program, for example, to be ideologically and practically unconnected to one another except by the student's presence while moving through the program: an educational psychology offering (with required classroom observations) here, a tutoring experience as part of a reading methods course there, and student teaching somewhere else. Few examples of programs that systematically attend to the relationships between these elements can be found in practice or in the research literature.

In perhaps even more dramatic fashion, inservice clinical teacher education seems to be driven by the fad of the moment.[44] Seldom seen are commitments to long-term, comprehensively envisioned inservice programs undergirded by principles and properties that frame the programs over time. Instead, teachers are confronted with sets of workshops that bear little conceptual or practical relationship to each other. Unfortunately, when attempts are made to provide coherence, those attempts are often only umbrellas under which any number of concepts, prescriptions, recommendations, and "workshops" huddle together. The latest one is "excellence."[45] Although it is difficult to argue against excellence as an ideal toward which we might all earnestly strive, it is difficult to conceive of any opportunity, no matter how loosely connected to the next, that would not fit.

The RITE framework requires that there be a strand of intention and activity that, over time and with concerted effort, guides a set of cumulative experiences aimed toward an articulated purpose. To require such continuity is to demand that clinical teacher education programs be thought of as long-term investments in teachers, teaching, schooling, and the advancement of the society. It is also to demand that the program be conceptualized and put forward with consideration given to its appeal to teachers and the degree to which that appeal will sustain participation over time. Here, of course, lies the rub. For an idea or a procedure or a new way of viewing teaching to "stick," it must be (for teacher education) uncharacteristically powerful. We know that teachers, like most adults, can learn to do almost anything. But we also know that teachers are more attracted to some ideas and practices than others. Part of the work of providing clinical teacher education is learning what is attractive, and another part is developing means to interest teachers in aspects of teaching that appear less attractive.

This last point may appear to be condescending. It is not meant to provide support for the argument that teachers "don't know what is good for them." It is meant to provide a stimulus for teacher educators, preservice and inservice, to discover and invent ways to act upon the conditions of teaching such that latent interests and concerns of teachers can be brought to the forefront of attention and used to promote growth and change. In the end, teacher education must be concerned with its appeal to teachers. In many schools, for instance, the conditions of work are such that it is no wonder that teachers resist or, at best, uneasily and reluctantly engage in professional development activity. Certain conditions militate against engagement, such as already crowded days, adult exchanges inhibited by schedules that must be followed, administrative refusal to provide release time for professional activity, the absence of a congenial space for adults to gather together over professional issues, and other roadblocks placed in the way of "excellence." It is when these and other negative context conditions are ameliorated that teachers will respond positively to the provision of clinical teacher education. And it is when these conditions are corrected that truly ongoing, sustained, and cumulative clinical teacher education can be put into place.

Clearly, in addition to offering a vision of what such an ongoing program should accomplish, we must also acknowledge that the support necessary for such efforts is considerable—support in terms of dollars, in terms of redistribution of scarce resources, and in terms of new ways of constructing teachers' workworlds. There is evidence, however, that the support for an ongoing set of meaningful professional growth opportunities is well repaid in terms of both improved teaching and more positive climates in classrooms and schools.

Feature #6: The program is developmental. The term *developmental* has been used by psychologists to refer to what can be called naturally occurring stages of growth, alterations in the ways that mind and body work as a consequence less of intervention than of the usual order of events. The RITE framework of clinical teacher education uses the term differently. Because we are concerned with the professional growth and change of teachers, we use the word *developmental* to suggest an orderly progression toward advanced professional status.[46] Although one can assume that young adults, for example, will grow in maturity as human beings, we take the view that teacher education programs can contribute to that growth in professional ways.

Naturally, the developmental feature of the RITE framework is aligned with the ongoing feature in its emphasis on a set of activities that, *over time,* are incremental, cumulative, and purposeful. In contrast, repetitive, unsequenced, unconnected teacher education opportunities are out of alignment with the RITE framework.

Three considerations are of particular importance in designing a program that is developmental. First, one must distinguish the various levels of professional growth. Second, teacher education programs should be designed according to these distinctions between levels. Third, developmental differences will affect appropriate sources of information for planning a teacher education program at every level.

The existence of levels or stages of professional growth has been well-documented.[47] We are aware of the distinctions that can be made between prospective teachers, new teachers, and career teachers. Recently, teacher education programs have begun to be guided by these distinctions, and perceptive observers of schools have helped to sort out conceptual and programmatic issues that clarify the various stages. For a number of years, the role of teacher and the acts of teaching have been viewed as relatively "flat" or uniform. That is, "a teacher is a teacher is a teacher." This position suggests that there are relatively few differentiators in quality or style. It promotes the notion that the new teacher should look, act, and think much like the career teacher, that student teachers should quickly make the transition toward that same look, and, importantly, that teachers should therefore be rewarded pretty much the same, although longevity and advanced degrees are typically used to provide greater rewards for the veteran than for the newcomer.

Research activity and political activity have made serious dents in that point of view. From a research perspective, we are more sharply aware of the distinctions between novices and experts, neophytes and longtermers, beginners and veterans.[48] Furthermore, we are aware of qualitative differences *within* these groups: Some newcomers are different from other newcomers, some veterans are more expert than others, and so on. These distinctions have meaning for the ways we think about and conduct teacher education programs.

The differences also have political and economic meaning. A current issue is the controversy over the selection and subsequent reward of so-called "master teachers."[49] To claim that this controversy is purely (or even mainly) intellectual is to miss the point. The claims for mastery for some and, one would assume, less-than-mastery for others call for differential rewards, real and ceremonial, and for radically different ways of going about the business of teaching and schooling. State legislatures, local school boards, teacher organizations, and other constituent groups are taking positions on the mastery issue right and left. Many of these positions are based more on political and economic viewpoints than on theoretical and rational proposals to stimulate mastery in teaching.

Notwithstanding the difficulties posed by within-group differences, we can and should attend to the distinctions between groups. Armed with the knowledge that people who have never taught are different from those who have taught for five or ten years, we can plan teacher education programs that take that issue into serious consideration, as well as plan programs that are inherently developmental themselves. Clinical teacher education programs can not only address the distinctions between initiates, neophytes, and veterans, but also sort out what it is to be a "successful" student of teaching. What are the most powerful influences in learning about teaching? In the same way, we can conceive of what it is to be a "successful" student teacher. What is it to be effective in a heavily supervised setting? And so on, through career teaching. Basically, in this aspect of the developmental feature of the RITE model, we demand that distinctions be made between career stages, and that those distinctions be in terms of expectations for success and effectiveness as well as in terms of the learning opportunities that are considered to be of greatest potential in accomplishing that success and effectiveness at each stage.[50] These considerations will, we believe, raise important questions about the "sameness" orientation that is too often applied across teachers as a group.

In terms of the developmental feature as a planning stance, the RITE framework requires that clinical teacher education programs be planned and implemented such that the various intentions and activities lead toward significantly more sophisticated consequences over time. For preservice teacher education, this might mean a reconsideration and strengthening of the "observe, tutor, teach small group, teach whole group, student-teach, teach all day, and teach all week" sequence that is typically spread over a two-year or longer period of time. For beginning teachers, it might mean a systematic assessment of the new teacher's role in the system and a gradual set of events that lead the person through that role and into career teacher status. For inservice education, it might mean a school system commitment to a conception of excellence and then, in the same way that a sound curriculum for children is planned, the formulation of a program presenting increasingly complex ways of demonstrating that excellence. (This is not to deny the importance of treating pressing issues and events that may not fall within the purview of the developmentally planned program. It is, however, meant to suggest that deviations that deflect attention from the developmental program must be considered seriously.)

One way to look at the developmental feature is to consider the degree of autonomy versus supervision that teachers enjoy during the course of a career. The prospective teacher in a college or university setting has little autonomy and is heavily supervised by professors. As the person moves into the first years of teaching, he or she is typically supervised by building and system officers but to a lesser extent than in a preservice program. Tenure and extended teaching experience are accompanied by greater autonomy of professional practice.

Such a complementary relationship of decreased supervision and increased autonomy over time must be based on decisions as to how that autonomy is exercised, what knowledge informs it, and what career goals guide it. Teachers, teacher educators, and school officials need to work together toward the implementation of clinical teacher education programs that capitalize on the teacher's growing autonomy such that it leads toward exemplary professional status.

It was suggested earlier that there are appropriate sources of information, knowledge, and skill for determining the focus of a developmental clinical teacher education program. Naturally, valued knowledge regarding teaching and schooling will be a primary guide. Two others are suggested. First, recent research regarding teacher development, its prospects and its pitfalls, can provide important information for planners. We know considerably more now than in past years about how teachers grow and change, how they think about their professional activity, and how they perceive problems and issues in their worlds.[51] This information can provide data for decisions both about purposes and about implementation.

Also, it has become apparent that many of the best ideas for improvement reside within the teaching ranks, especially among career teachers.[52] One approach to development is to systematically and rigorously assess the status of teaching and teachers in a school or a system. By status, we mean not just deficiencies that can be noted and verified, but also widely-held concerns about the conditions of schooling, modes of instruction, roles of teachers, outcomes of instruction, and so on. This assessment approach is guided, of course, by one of the most time-honored maxims regarding teaching children and youth: "Start from where they are." Why not do the same with teachers? By designing clinical teacher education programs that are responsive to the development levels (pedagogical and institutional rather than psychological and physical) of teachers, the program can capitalize upon vested interests and realize the true value of its human capital.

Feature #7: The program is analytic and reflective. Naive observers of classrooms and schools often comment on the helter-skelter human activity they see. Children are moving; teachers are moving; materials are distributed and collected; whole groups shift from one place in the building to another. Although teachers and other educators may agree that the activity is purposeful, our patrons sometimes conclude that this is a confusing and uncertain state of affairs. There *is* a certain "busyness" about teaching and schooling. The students arrive more or less on cue, and the next five or six hours are characterized by a variety of interactions between those students and their teachers. In fact, it is this "meeting with students" that is most often central to any characterization of teaching as professional activity. Put another way, teaching is most often defined by teacher-student interaction.

There is, however, a more comprehensive view of teachers and teaching. According to this view, teachers engage in a number of important activities that take place apart from students. They plan; they diagnose; they evaluate; they learn from experts; they attend graduate school.[53] The RITE framework of clinical teacher education requires of professional development programs that time and space be set aside for the purposes of analysis and reflection, important intellectual activities that affect how one carries out one's professional role.

This feature, analysis and reflection, may at first glance seem a departure from our stance regarding the centrality of context to the RITE framework. Such is not the case. Too often, it appears, the time that teachers spend away from classrooms and schools, physically and emotionally/psychologically, is time that is purposefully divorced from consideration of those workplaces. Teachers attend classes in colleges and universities frequently devoted to issues dramatically unrelated to the realities of their professional worlds. There is, in effect, a distancing of the analytic and reflective aspects of teachers' lives that dilutes the power of those activities to alter life in classrooms. (Of course, it is important to engage in topics other than classrooms and schools. But to almost completely divorce the objects of study from what teachers regularly *do* is, we think, a serious error in judgment.)

It has long been hypothesized that reflecting upon one's activities is a powerful way to increase professional authority and effectiveness.[54] Furthermore, reflection is believed to improve the professional's ability to characterize and thus influence his or her ways of thinking about and acting upon the self in relation to others he or she encounters. In fact, teachers often become so caught up in their workworlds that they either choose to avoid reflection or are forced to do so in deference to the demands of classrooms and schools. Yet, there is evidence that teachers who regularly analyze and think about their professional activity are more perceptive and influential teachers.[55]

Lest it be thought that the RITE framework is promoting the monastic contemplative life for teachers, we hasten to point out that this emphasis on analysis and reflection is meant to guide the development and implementation of exemplary clinical teacher education programs. The effective clinical program will have as a primary component the opportunity for participants, whether prospective teachers or teachers in service, to think about what they do in relation to their teaching activity and in relation to the teacher education program itself. The framework, then, calls for examination of self in relation to school and classroom contexts *and* self in relation to experiences in clinical teacher education programs.

This feature of the framework would preclude the "do-it-by-the-numbers" form of teacher education—the obligatory one-shot workshop, the no-follow-up lecture by a visiting dignitary, and so on. It would require that there be systematic allocations of time for individuals to reflect upon their experiences, alone and together, for the purpose of making those experiences more meaningful as well as for the purpose of raising important questions about the nature of meaning in experience.

CONCLUSION

This chapter has suggested a framework for clinical teacher education that may be put to use in programs designed for prospective teachers, beginning teachers, and career teachers. The framework proposes context as a defining property and a set of seven critical features that are believed central to the enactment of sound clinical teacher education. Furthermore, the framework is based upon the strong belief that the best clinical teacher education programs will give attention to the defining property and all of the critical features in interaction.

Using this framework would cause teacher educators, preservice and inservice, to develop programs with clearly stated and public purposes. Such programs would be based on a conception of teacher growth and improvement that is grounded in an understanding of the issues and problems of teachers' relationships in their classrooms and schools, guided by a conception of cumulative experience and power over time, rooted in a substantial and verifiable knowledge base, and sensitive to the ways that participants think about and reflect upon both the program and the places in which the teachers do their work.

The nation, some say, is "at risk."[56] We are not certain that this general conclusion is warranted by the assumptions that led to it in some commission reports, scholarly pronouncements, and studies of schools. We are, however, concerned about the "at-risk" status of the nation in special terms of its teachers and their work in schools. If we want to move from a nation of "knowers of facts" to a nation of "problem-solvers," from a conception of educational opportunity based on opportunism to one that leads citizens to discover the "good life," from a culture that undervalues the significant experiment in universal education to one that supports that enterprise, then we must work toward the intellectual and practical empowerment of teachers. One part of that important endeavor is the enactment of improved opportunities for teachers to become what we all know they want to be: thoughtful, effective, *excellent* professionals.

2

The RITE Framework of Teacher Education: Preservice Applications

Willis D. Copeland

In one of the colloquia that reviewed an early draft of Chapter 1, a supervisor of student teachers asked, "What is in this conceptual thing that really helps teacher educators help teachers?" An appropriate question, indeed. In this and the next two chapters, we propose to provide answers to that question in such a way that teacher educators can determine how this "conceptual thing" can be incarnated in the programs they offer. Our purpose is to fill in, by description and example, the outline of RITE clinical teacher education offered in Chapter 1 so that teacher educators can reasonably answer such questions as these: "Are the things that we are now doing really consistent with RITE clinical teacher education?" "If they are not, should they be? What are the costs and benefits?" and "What is necessary to properly implement the RITE clinical framework of teacher education in our program?"

THE IDEAL TEACHER AND THE NOVICE

Early in Chapter 1, a description of the ideal teacher is offered. Such an approach is reasonable. The reader would expect that any volume which proposes, as this one does, to suggest changes in the processes for producing a product should justify those changes in terms of desired qualities of the product to be produced.

In this chapter, this RITE conception of the ideal teacher must be modified as a goal of preservice teacher education. One cannot assume nor expect that newly credentialed teachers will possess all the qualities and capabilities of the ideal teacher. Those qualities and capabilities normally result from years of experience and professional training. Experienced teachers almost universally attest to the tremendous strides they made during their first years of teaching. Later chapters in this volume will explore the significant educational paths along which such teachers trek as they approach the status of the ideal teacher.

In accordance with the RITE framework of clinical teacher education, we propose that preservice teacher education programs define themselves as producers of *novice teachers*, beginners who have been appropriately prepared in their credentialing experience to be poised on the threshold of a productive teaching career.[1]

Many individuals in teaching and teacher education would not accept this proposition. Cooperating teachers often lament that teacher education students who come to them for student teaching are not prepared to function in the classroom as effective teachers should.[2] Personnel directors in school districts commonly consign first-year teachers to positions that would severely test the most experienced and capable teacher. Inservice coordinators seldom offer beginning teachers training or support that differs in any significant way from that offered to their colleagues with twenty years' experience.

Nevertheless, a basic assumption of the RITE framework for clinical teacher education is that teaching excellence derives from a continuing process of personal and professional growth which extends over the career of the teacher. Preservice teacher education offers the first systematic steps in that process and is appropriately shaped by an understanding of what its legitimate goals are within the larger process of developing the ideal teacher defined in Chapter 1.

What would such a novice teacher look like? Joyce and Clift suggest that credentialed graduates should be prepared to undertake a lifelong study of the world and of self, of academic knowledge, and of the task of teaching. They should be able to participate in efforts to adopt innovations toward the improvement of schools, and they should be able to approach the generic problems of the classroom and school in which they work.[3]

This view of a good graduate of a preservice teacher education program is consistent with the RITE framework of teacher education. In both views two qualities are emphasized: basic capabilities and predisposition for professional growth.

Basic capabilities. Like the ideal teacher described in Chapter 1, the novice teacher should be required to possess basic capabilities for establishing classroom environments that are "orderly, friendly, attractive, and, with occasional planned exceptions, academically purposeful" (p. 5). Pupils should not suffer at the hands of first-year teachers. Yet the novice teacher cannot be expected to demonstrate the extensive professional skills typical of his or her experienced colleagues. As an example, it may not be appropriate to expect the newly credentialed graduate to work efficiently and skillfully with the widest variety of pupils, including those with extremely unusual and special needs. Years of experience and focused professional training may be necessary before a teacher could be considered capable of productively offering a fully mainstreamed educational program in the regular classroom.

The ideal teacher described in Chapter 1 is "aware of a set of options for delivering subject matter so that effective, efficient, and long-term learning takes place" (p. 5). Obviously, the set of options available to the experienced teacher should be extensive and should have been refined and augmented over the period of his or her professional career. Just as obviously, those options on which the novice teacher is able to act will be much less numerous. Yet, they must be sufficient to allow the teacher to be functional in standard classroom settings. Intelligent use of a rich variety of instructional strategies and techniques will come to the novice teacher with time, experience, and purposeful professional development.

Predisposition for professional growth. In acknowledging these limitations to the novice teacher's capabilities, one assumes they will be overcome. A second quality of a graduate of a good teacher credential program should be the predisposition to embark upon a career-long process of learning, refinement, experiment, and change.[4] Novice teachers should be empowered by their professional training to explore alternatives, weigh their values in terms of potential instructional ends in the classroom, decide what teaching and learning behaviors are most appropriate, and act on those decisions.

The task, then, is to educate novice teachers so that they acquire both the basic teaching capabilities necessary for beginning teaching and the predisposition for learning to teach crucial to their continuing professional development. This chapter suggests that such education can best be accomplished within a full-time program of professional preparation that is conducted cooperatively by an institution of higher education and a group of local schools, and that manifests the seven critical features of the RITE framework for clinical teacher education described in Chapter 1: It must be context-related, purposeful and articulated, participatory and collaborative, knowledge-based, ongoing, developmental, and analytic and reflective.

A PROGRAM OF PROFESSIONAL TEACHER PREPARATION

The RITE framework of clinical teacher education is defined primarily by the context of living classrooms, which brings meaning and substance to the professional development of beginning teachers. Thus, the apparent focus of clinical teacher education would be those components of the teacher education program—early field experiences and student teaching—which are based in school classrooms. Such a focus is only partially appropriate. While these field-based components clearly are crucial, development of a clinical teacher education program based on the RITE framework also includes consideration of the other components of a teacher education program—foundations courses, general and special methods courses, pre-student-teaching laboratory experiences—whenever connections can be made between them and the student teacher's field-based experiences.

Furthermore, and this point cannot be made too strongly, in a clinical teacher education program that reflects the RITE framework, such connections between campus- and field-based components are deliberate, strong, and numerous. Like sinews connecting the living body, common themes, examples, requirements, and recommendations run through all components of the program. Ideas from research on teaching behavior introduced in an educational psychology course require demonstration in a methods course, observation in a field setting, exploration in a simulation laboratory, and practice in student teaching. Specifics of a conference with parents during student teaching need to be related to principles and values explored during a social foundations course.

Admittedly, recognition of the need for such connections is not new. Most competent teacher educators have often considered the desirability of connecting learning. The difficulty is in the connecting. The establishment and nurture of connections that organize effort and focus it on definite purposes has not been common in teacher education. The following sections will use the "conceptual thing" that is the RITE framework to develop examples of how such connections can be made and how the concepts that shape the RITE framework can be used to inform the development of a teacher education program aimed at producing truly capable novice teachers.

A caution is in order, however. Because of the wide diversity of contexts within which teacher education takes place, it would be inappropriate in these pages to recommend an ideal teacher education program. The reader is invited, instead, to take what is presented here as example, to integrate with it his or her experience, and to use it to consider the utility of the RITE framework for shaping his or her own teacher education program.

BUILDING A TEACHING REPERTOIRE

The recommendations that student teachers receive and act on may offer a useful ingress for exploring the character that a teacher education program would assume if it reflected the concepts of the RITE framework of clinical teacher education. It is common for student teachers to act on how-to-teach recommendations received from others. Some recommendations are presented in very formal ways, via lectures and demonstrations in university classroom methods courses or descriptions offered by experienced teachers of actions they consider appropriate in various situations. Other recommendations, such as passing remarks from fellow student teachers, come informally. Still others arrive very indirectly, from observing experienced teachers at work with pupils or even from working with pupils themselves.[5]

However they are made, recommendations concerning professional behavior clearly play a large part in any teacher education program. Student teachers expect to be taught how to teach well. Cooperating teachers often strive to help their student teachers acquire those techniques that have been successful for them. Whole training technologies, built around exhibition of models of desired teaching behavior and opportunities to practice in controlled conditions with immediate feedback—often via videotape—have been implemented to encourage acquisition of recommended behaviors.

Yet, it is an unfortunate fact that complaints about the lack of consistency in the recommendations received from various components of teacher education programs are common among both credential students and graduated teachers.[6] During one of the colloquia that contributed to the preparation of this volume, a cooperating teacher characterized her student teacher as being "caught and pummeled between the demands of the university and the realities of the classroom."

Such inconsistency in recommendations may derive from the lack of a set of assumptions, goals, and values concerning teaching, pupils, and learning that is shared across the program. Indeed, a RITE study of preservice programs found remarkably few explicit statements—much less agreements—concerning program goals on which one might expect recommendations to be based.[7]

At the very time that this condition of inconsistency is being brought to light, policymakers are intensifying their insistence that teacher training institutions increase the effectiveness with which they prohibit incapable teachers from entering the profession. Reinforcing the institution's gatekeeping function would appear impossible in the absence of a clearly articulated set of purposes that guide programmatic decisions within the institution.

REDUCING CONFLICT BETWEEN
THE CAMPUS AND THE FIELD

A program that reflects the RITE framework of clinical teacher education is *purposeful and articulated*. That is, programmatic decisions, components, and their relationships are publicly and apparently informed by the program's purposes, goals, and values. The program's members—faculty, field supervisors, cooperating teachers, and students—all share an understanding of the program's articulated purposes and how the program's components are arrayed to meet those purposes. Under such a condition, recommendations to the student teachers from whatever source in the program would be consistent and appropriate. The possibility of conflict between recommendations from the campus and the field would be reduced.

During the RITE preservice colloquium, a cooperating teacher confessed, "My biggest problem is determining what I should do with my student teacher." Such a statement clearly indicates a lack of shared understanding with the institution that placed the student teacher in her classroom concerning purposes and the plans for achieving them. As a result, the teacher is unsure of what recommendations she should make to the student teacher and of how they should be made.

Some programs attempt to solve this problem by communicating to cooperating teachers, often via a handbook or a beginning-of-the-year meeting, the program's purposes, methods, and expectations. Such an approach is insufficient for a clinical teacher education program based on the RITE framework. It implies that the program's key task is to confer on cooperating teachers an understanding of the program. It casts cooperating teachers in the role of consumers when they are more properly allied with other program components as *producers* of student teachers.

The development of a purposeful and articulated program requires the program's members, including the cooperating teachers, to work together in a *participatory and collaborative* manner. Clear agreements concerning purposes, methods, and a language to communicate them are to be shared by all members of the program. The implication here is that cooperating teachers, who have traditionally been assigned the role of "worker bees" in teacher education programs, now be involved in policy discussions concerning all aspects of the program, including purposes, course content, and program structure.

An example of such collaboration might be of help here. When the decision was made to reformulate the credential program in secondary social science at one teacher education institution, the methods course professor intended to identify a set of what she called "instructional strategies" to be taught to the students. Though the professor in the methods course had a good idea of what strategies she would choose, she avoided simply making the choices and constituting her course accordingly. Instead, she undertook an extensive collaborative effort by convening a series of meetings attended by the university's field supervisors, the professor of the psychological foundations class, and eight representatives of the cooperating teachers with whom the credential students were to be placed during student teaching.

In the early meetings, a considerable amount of time was consumed in developing a common language and familiarizing the group with the notion of instructional strategies and with various examples currently in the literature. The group eventually identified a set of strategies with which all agreed student teachers should be familiar. The list was similar but not identical to the one the methods course professor would have generated alone. Although each cooperating teacher and field supervisor was initially unfamiliar with one or more of the strategies on the list, by the end of the series of meetings all had a working knowledge of each strategy.

But the group went further. It developed a format for assignments that required student teachers to plan and teach lessons based on a selection of the strategies. The psychological foundations professor agreed to make the psychological principles underlying the strategies a major focus of his course. The field supervisors organized a pre-student-teaching peer teaching experience in which the student teachers were given an opportunity to practice the strategies in a controlled setting. The cooperating teachers planned a series of inservice workshops to teach their colleagues the strategies. The workshops were taught by two cooperating teachers, a field supervisor, and the methods course professor. The psychological foundations professor volunteered as a guest speaker. The methods course professor invited selected cooperating teachers to serve as guest speakers in the methods course, where they presented examples of the strategies in use in their own classrooms. The university agreed to increase the compensation, provide free library cards, and offer discounts to basketball games for cooperating teachers who attended the workshops.

Initiating changes with this degree of collaboration among such diverse program principals was admittedly difficult. The payoff, however, was a great reduction in the student teachers' sense of incongruence between the campus and the schools. The focus shifted from "Should I really have to do this?" to "How well am I doing it?" Compared with those in other secondary subject area programs in the same institution, the social studies student teachers expressed a clearer understanding of the purposes of the program and of the relationships between its components.[8]

The above example illustrates the importance of another concept in the RITE framework: The decisions made by the group proceeded from a *knowledge base* that, by virtue of the early meetings, was shared by the program principals. This knowledge base initially was represented to the group by the methods course professor, but the group members quickly undertook to assimilate the knowledge — that is, to seek out and identify examples from their own professional work of the strategies in use and to relate the strategies to additional possibilities within their curriculum. Knowledge developed via educational research was thus allowed to interact with craft knowledge accumulated by the teachers in the course of their careers, and, as a result of this interaction, the knowledge base available to the program was broadened. The principals in this social studies teacher education program evolved the ability to make use of commonly-owned knowledge that allowed a clearer focus on the program's articulated purposes and facilitated a consistency in recommendations directed to the student teachers.

ATTENTION TO THE CONTEXT OF
A CLINICAL TEACHER EDUCATION PROGRAM

As was emphasized in Chapter 1, "the hallmark of a clinical teacher education program is its relation to the context in which it is carried forward" (p. 7). Consideration of *context* at the preservice level is particularly important from a number of perspectives.

First, the program must ensure that the context within which a student is placed to practice-teach is one that will support the student's professional development. One characteristic of such a context is that it offers a sound educational experience for its pupils. Schools that do not do this are simply not appropriate settings for clinical teacher education. A context where pupils experience sound educational practices is vital to preservice teacher preparation for at least two reasons. First, models of appropriate professional behavior within the context must be sufficiently numerous. Such models are essential for the professional development of new teachers. Second, the behavior of the context's constituents — its pupils, cooperating teacher, principal, parents, etc. — should provide feedback which shapes the student teacher's actions in appropriate ways. For example, a student teacher's appropriate use of concept attainment strategy would be rewarded by the positive responses of pupils if they were accustomed to teacher use of that strategy throughout the year.

One cannot assume, however, that a school that provides a very good education to its pupils necessarily also offers an appropriate context for preparing student teachers. Another key characteristic of contexts appropriate for teacher education is the school staff's commitment to the preparation of future professionals. Not all good teachers share such a commitment, nor should they. Indeed, Little found that although some strong school faculties provide very well for the learning of pupils in their schools, their very strength, cohesiveness, and commitment to teaching militate against a successful entrance into the school by neophyte student teachers.[9] Results from the RITE study and other similar research suggest, on the other hand, that those who are committed to work with student teachers in clinical teacher education programs manifest their commitment in a number of specific ways. They are willing to work closely with student teachers, offering advice and coaching that support transfer of learning from other program components to the student teaching setting.[10] They do not assume a student teacher's readiness to perform all teaching functions, but instead adjust the experience to the student teacher's actual level of development. They delegate responsibility to the student teacher in appropriate degree, recognizing that responsibility includes the right to make decisions and have a degree of control over circumstances. They support the student teacher's formation of his or her teaching style instead of insisting on adoption of their own styles. Finally, they offer both specific models of behaviors, teaching techniques, and attitudes that they recommend to the student teacher, and a more general model of a professional who practices self-reflection as an active learner and thus continues to grow as an expert teacher.[11]

In a clinical teacher education program, the context supports the program's recommendations. The power of the context to shape teacher behavior has been documented in a variety of settings.[12] Such research suggests that when a program recommends particular teaching behaviors that are not characteristic of the context in which the student is directed to practice them, the student's success is threatened.

Here is an illustration: A student teacher in a social studies education program would be taught in his methods course a strategy for conducting discussions about controversial issues. However effective that methods instruction might be, if he attempted to use the strategy in a classroom in which no controversial issues had been raised during the preceding year, in which the cooperating teacher's dominant method of teaching was lecturing, and in which pupils were unaccustomed to speaking without being called on, his success would be in doubt. The context would not support or respond to the teaching behaviors required of the new strategy.

Fortunately, the sample social studies training program described earlier is attempting to attend to this context effect. The participation of cooperating teachers in the initial identification of teaching strategies and the follow-up inservice training of cooperating teachers in the use of those strategies are intended to shape the context so that it better supports the purposes of the program. When pupils are accustomed to the use of particular teaching strategies throughout the school year by their own teachers, the student teacher's use of the strategy will likely meet a more supportive reception, and the student's success will thus depend more on his or her particular facility with the strategy than on the fit between the strategy and the context.

A clinical teacher education program promotes the student teacher's ability to understand the context. The context within which preservice clinical teacher education is pursued is important from a second perspective. Not only should the context be supportive of the purposes of the program, but the student teacher should acquire facility at understanding the context and responding to it intelligently. Continued reference to the context should become a practiced and almost habitual element of the student teacher's decision-making processes. In the above example, student teachers are not required to use all the strategies learned in their methods course. As it is unreasonable to expect that a cooperating teacher would choose to use all the strategies in his or her own teaching, it would be just as unreasonable to require the student teacher to force all the strategies into his or her teaching experience. Instead, the student is assigned the task of choosing from the strategies offered those most appropriate for the subject matter, for the student's own emerging style of teaching, and — most pertinent to the present discussion — for the pupils he or she is teaching. Such choices, when purposefully approached and carefully coached by the university supervisor and the cooperating teacher, give the student teacher the opportunity to practice attending consciously to the context and its influence on teaching and learning.

As this practice in attending to the context and its influence on teaching continues, the student establishes relationships between the context and the knowledge base about which he or she is learning and on which the clinical teacher education program is founded. The pedagogical content explored in campus-based courses such as the methods course described above takes on significance as the student uses it to build meaning about teaching within the classroom context. Thus, to the extent that the student establishes for him- or herself these relationships between the campus-acquired content and the field-based experience, the program's knowledge base actually becomes a part of the context within which the student is working. This knowledge becomes a resource to be assessed and processed for understanding, just as pupil behavior, cooperating teacher models and suggestions, physical characteristics of the classroom, and school-wide norms of teacher behavior — all components of the context for learning to teach — are assessed and processed. The clinical teacher education program is characterized by a large number of potential relationships between the knowledge base it uses and the context within which teacher education proceeds, and by the presence of consciously designed activities that encourage student teachers to perceive and explore these relationships as they build their professional teaching capabilities.

Clinical teacher education programs enable the student teacher to act on the context. Context is important to clinical teacher education from a third perspective. The argument was made above that context is a strong determinant of teaching behavior and that the use of teaching behaviors not supported by the context is problematic. That argument must now be moderated. Professional teachers must have the capability for acting beyond mere accommodation to the context. To be successful, they must actively shape the context to better support the learning they propose for their pupils. Therefore, an important goal of a clinical teacher education program is for its student teachers to acquire tools useful in changing the context. Furthermore, they should be afforded the opportunity to use those tools as they practice shaping the context within which they work. Such practice depends heavily on the *developmental* status of the student teacher and his or her ability to engage in *analytic and reflective* activities. Both of these concepts will be discussed in detail below.

The characteristics of clinical teacher education often demonstrate strong interactions. By nature, the seven characteristics of clinical teacher education offered in the RITE framework do not stand alone. Rather, these characteristics support and define one another. They are a loosely braided rug in which individual strands of different colors and textures interact to give form to the whole.

As an example, the process of collaboration in the social studies program described above produced a benefit that the methods course professor had not anticipated. Her initial intent was to put forth as a program *purpose* a set of strategies that could be consistently recommended across the program and would thus have a greater likelihood of being adopted by student teachers. Her technique was to use a process of *collaboration* to develop that set of strategies from a knowledge base. Recommendations to student teachers do not, however, assume validity simply because they represent an articulation of a program's purposes that is shared by the program's principal personnel. An additional important characteristic of clinical teacher education bears on what recommendations are offered: Good professional preparation of teachers is *developmental*.

The development of student teachers' academic, professional, and personal needs over the time of preservice preparation is becoming more clearly understood.[13] The RITE framework of clinical teacher education suggests that understanding of this development be used to temper the recommendations given the student teacher with an assessment of that student teacher's developing needs and concerns.

Inquiry teaching was a favorite strategy of the methods professor in the above example. In her course she had, in previous years, given student teachers descriptions and even shown them films of active classrooms with pupils eagerly generating and testing alternative hypotheses to social and historical problems. Her recommendation to the student teachers had clearly been to give secondary pupils fewer answers and more time to pursue and test answers for themselves.

Such a recommendation, standing alone, is certainly laudable, for it reflects an orientation toward some of education's most worthy goals. Most educators would agree that a learner should be cast in the active role of seeker after knowledge rather than the passive role of knowledge recipient. Yet, if a student teacher's developmental needs are a valued element of the teacher education program, and if a student teacher has just begun an assignment, is unsure of him- or herself, and has not yet established a history of successfully managing large-group learning situations, a recommendation to engage in inquiry teaching may be entirely inappropriate.

During the course of the meetings described above, the cooperating teachers talked of the early needs that, in previous years, they had observed developing in their student teachers. They suggested that the methods course professor review the advisability of recommending the inquiry strategy early in the student teaching program or to a student teacher who was experiencing difficulty with classroom management. Now, many methods texts emphasize inquiry. Various educators and others are now calling for instruction in the "higher level thinking skills" that inquiry proposes to promote. For these reasons, and possibly also because she likes it, the professor had made inquiry an important component of her methods course. Yet, in the light of developmental considerations, she came to understand that some student teachers might not be able to take the professor's recommendation and act on it as she intended. When clinical teacher education calls attention to the developmental aspect of preparing new teachers, it forces reconsideration of the content of credential programs: What is the nature of the early needs of beginning teachers? How do those needs change as the student matures professionally? How are those needs best met at each stage of the progress towards earning one's credentials?

Another example of the developmental nature of preservice clinical teacher education may be in order here. Throughout the literature on the nature of the relationship between a supervisor and a teacher, there is a tendency to support a non-directive stance by the supervisor. That is, the supervisor is supposed to assume the facilitating role of trusted colleague—helping the teacher to define questions about his or her teaching and the pupils' learning, to check perceptions of classroom occurrences, and to test hypotheses about proposals for improvement. Though most of this literature is directed at work with experienced teachers, there may be a tendency among supervisors of student teachers to adopt the recommended non-directive stance. Yet, some evidence suggests that beginning student teachers prefer much more directive intervention from their supervisors.[14] They welcome criticism, praise, suggestions, and ideas, and they have little patience when their own questions are reflected back to them without answer. There is also evidence that this need for direction may moderate over time and that, toward the end of the student teaching experience, student teachers grow more willing to receive non-directive supervision as their own confidence and ability develop. The point is that the behavior of supervisors, like many other components of a clinical teacher education program, should be tuned to the developmental needs of the student teacher.

This discussion appears to place the teacher education program in a difficult position. On the one hand, the program should articulate and make public its purposes so that the recommendations offered to student teachers are consistent. At the same time, the program should be a bellwether, subject to the developing needs of its student teachers. How can one assume both positions? The answer is that *one* cannot.

A clinical teacher education program is developed via a collaborative process. A clinical teacher education program based on the RITE framework, by virtue of being *participatory and collaborative*, engages all its principal participants, including the student teachers, in its formative processes. Mechanisms such as problem discussion groups and conferences of staff and students are created to enable communication between all program participants. These mechanisms are used by the staff to inform the students of the purposes of the program and the methods used by the program to fulfill those purposes. Special emphasis is placed on the program's attempts to match content and experiences with student needs.

The mechanisms are also useful to the students in at least two ways. First, they enable the students to voice their own needs and concerns. Not only does this allow the program staff the opportunity to react and be responsive to the student's needs, but also it reduces the student's anxiety by reducing individual isolation and revealing that their own private concerns are often shared by others and may be, in fact, less troublesome or even catastrophic than they had previously assumed.

A second useful product of these mechanisms of communication is that they reinforce for the student teacher the value of collaboration and participation among professionals. In this case, the medium is the message. Students experience and learn to value the process of making their individual concerns public and of seeking outside aid in pursuing solutions.

In a clinical teacher education program based on the RITE framework, cooperating teachers also enlist student teachers as collaborators in the classroom, giving them an increasing measure of responsibility ". . . to make decisions and have a degree of control over circumstances as well as acceptance of blame."[15]

A word of clarification is needed at this point about the nature of the participation and collaboration of student teachers in a preservice clinical teacher education program. The autonomy of professional teachers and its variation across stages of the teacher's career are discussed in the opening chapter of this volume. The observation is made that experienced teachers, by virtue of their greater expertise acquired over a career of professional development, legitimately exercise considerable autonomy in both their professional behavior as teachers and their continued professional education.

By contrast, student teachers enjoy less autonomy. They work within boundaries established by the program faculty, their supervisors, and their cooperating teachers. Yet, a central goal of RITE clinical teacher education at any stage is to increase the level of autonomy at which the teacher is able to function effectively. We emphasize both the desirability of giving student teachers initial experiences in collaboration on which future professional behavior can be built, and the usefulness of such collaboration in attending to the developing professional needs of student teachers.

BUILDING AN APPROACH TO
PROFESSIONAL DEVELOPMENT

Throughout the above discussion the construct of "recommendations" has been used as an ingress to allow exploration of the character that a teacher education program might assume if it reflected the concepts of the RITE framework of clinical teacher education. To this point, the focus has been on how-to-teach recommendations—that is, communications received by the student teacher concerning what is appropriate teaching behavior. Such recommendations, however, comprise a limited subset of those recommendations received by student teachers in a program characterized by the RITE framework. In addition to how-to-teach, such a program offers strong and consistent recommendations concerning how-to-be-a-teacher.

The distinction is not trivial. Whether how-to-teach recommendations emerge from that portion of the knowledge base that has evolved from a tradition-born craft in which experienced practitioners pass on career-accumulated knowledge to the apprentice, or whether they are derived from those parts of the knowledge base that are empirically grounded or theoretically supported, the emphasis is on acceptance, by the student teacher, of externally validated teaching actions. By contrast, the RITE framework casts teaching as a process of testing for the best match between instructional implementation and educational outcomes. Thus, a large subset of recommendations received by students in a RITE clinical teacher education program relate to how the teacher carries on the process of inquiry by which the match between the act of teaching and the goals of education can be tested.[16]

This orientation of how-to-be-a-teacher derives from the work of the RITE project and of a number of other researchers in teacher education.[17] It is expressed in the RITE framework's emphasis on the *analytic and reflective* component of teaching.

Central to this emphasis on analysis and reflection is the proposition that teaching is problematic. The basic how-to-be-a-teacher recommendation proposed by a clinical teacher education program based on the RITE framework is that the student approach the task of teaching by "... rendering problematic or questionable those aspects of teaching generally taken for granted."[18] At issue here is the student's basic conception of self as professional. The capable teacher is pictured as more than a competent technician, skillful in the application of a variety of teaching competencies recommended by others. A capable teacher is an inquirer who requires continuing reaffirmation of the utility of instructional behaviors.

Targets for analysis and reflection. When building a clinical teacher education program, teacher educators appropriately ask themselves what the target of their students' inquiry ought to be. Alan R. Tom points out that "... while there is consensus that the making of some aspect of teaching problematic is to question that which is taken for granted, no consensus exists concerning which aspects of teaching ought to be the object of problematic thinking."[19] He reviews the position of a number of teacher educators and proposes to array them along a continuum. At one end would be those who would cast the choice of teaching strategies as problematic while holding the objectives of teaching constant. At the other would be those who focus on a consideration of the problematic nature of the goals of education as a priori to a consideration of strategies for attaining those goals.[20]

Tom's distinction between these positions is no mere academic exercise. Its utility for guiding decisions concerning preservice teacher education emerges when we again consider the developmental aspects of clinical teacher education. It may be that the complexities involved in rendering problematic the ends of education as well as its means are beyond the abilities of the beginning credential candidate. For these students, inquiry into ends-means relationships may be most profitably pursued by holding ends as given and questioning the means by which they are reached.

This position has a very practical advantage when one considers how little discretionary power student teachers typically have over the establishment of educational goals in the classrooms in which they teach. At the same time, practicality notwithstanding, Kenneth Zeichner's suggestion that the targets of teachers' inquiry should include the goals of education as well as its means should not be dismissed (see Chapter 5). Though developing concerns may require that review of the appropriateness of educational goals be emphasized in the induction and inservice phases of teacher education, initial consideration of goals and preparation for their review would appear to be appropriate at the preservice level. The final balance struck by program designers over this issue is dependent on a number of factors including the intellectual and professional development of the student teacher, the potential responsiveness of the student teaching environment to the review of goals as well as methods, and the type of induction and inservice activities in which the program's student teachers are likely to enroll after employment.

Encouragement of analytic and reflective capabilities. At least four practices for encouraging the growth of analytic and reflective capabilities in students might be used in clinical teacher education programs. First, assignments may be made that link campus-based foundations courses with early field experiences and that require students to examine, review, or reflect on what they observe or experience in classrooms.[21] Here, foundations courses can provide students with lenses useful for detecting classroom phenomena not apparent to the untrained eye. Different sets of lenses can allow students to focus on phenomenal clusters such as child development, classroom management, relationships between instructional methods and outcomes, and unintended outcomes or the "hidden curriculum." Education students can be provided with specific targets for observation, such as the behavior of an individual pupil; the pupil monitoring behaviors, questioning tactics, or reinforcement techniques of an experienced teacher; or a pupil's use of ancillary instructional materials. To aid in this observation, students can be taught to use selected observation instruments that focus on the specific target. In addition, they can be asked to write interpretive descriptions of what they observe and to share those descriptions in class for the purpose of developing and testing generalizations about teaching and learning phenomena.

Assignments can also be completed during student teaching which foster an analytic and reflective stance toward the classroom. Perhaps the most common type of assignment here is a journal in which students record thoughts about their experiences. At least two requirements must be met for journal writing to be a valuable experience for student teachers. First is initial training that enables the students to undertake the thoughtful keeping of a journal. In this training they learn both the mechanics of journal writing — when and where to do it — and techniques such as what questions to ask themselves, how to focus on feelings and experiences, and how to make meaning out of them.

Second, journal writing requires regular and repeated feedback from at least one program staff member who offers reactions and encouragement to further insight. This last requirement is time-intensive but deemed essential by those who have successfully included journal writing in their programs as an effort to promote analysis and reflection in student teachers.

A second technique for promoting analytic and reflective capabilities is exhibition by the program staff of appropriate models of analysis and reflection. It is widely claimed that teacher education faculty tend not to model the teaching behavior they advocate.[22] Teachers are fond of recalling the methods course instructor who lectured on how to lead a discussion. These complaints of the lack of models are typically focused on teaching behavior, but can be extended here to instructional inquiry. Faculty members in a clinical teacher education program based on the RITE framework will often raise for consideration in class the subject of their own teaching. They will demonstrate, by their actions, attitudes that support analysis of and reflection about their own instructional behavior in campus-based as well as field-based courses. During the course they will seek student feedback and discuss its implications. They will invite examination of the worth of newly-tried class activities. If they decide upon changes, those changes will be described and their implications discussed so as to reveal a process of dynamic and formative change that shapes the course as it proceeds through the semester. Beginning teachers will thus be able to see their teacher education faculty function as students of their own teaching.

This emphasis on offering models of analysis and reflection is carried into the student teaching classroom as well. Barnes and Edwards describe cooperating teachers in more effective settings as being more willing to practice self-reflection as active learners and to use positive problem-solving approaches in most situations.[23]

A third technique for encouraging the growth of analytic and reflective capabilities in student teachers is individual intervention by program staff. This intervention is typically aimed at stimulating the analysis of relationships between educational methods and goals. Student teachers are encouraged to review their own actions and those of their pupils, to speculate about interrelationships, and to develop and test hypotheses relating to changes in their teaching behavior and changes in pupils' learning behavior that might result.

One framework for making such interventions is offered by the literature on clinical supervision.[24] The goal of clinical supervision is analysis, manipulation, and testing of the relationships between teaching and pupil behaviors—exactly the type of analysis and reflection the RITE framework of clinical teacher education intends to promote. The techniques used in clinical supervision are the individual planning conference between supervisor and teacher, focused observation of the teacher at work in the classroom, and the feedback conference in which observational data are used to generate and test hypotheses concerning change. One RITE study found that cooperating teachers in "more effective student teaching settings" tended to adopt the role of colleague with their student teachers, discussing and explaining alternatives rather than telling the student teacher what to do.[25] Such collaborative behavior is characteristic of clinical supervision and has been successfully used to promote analysis and reflection with student teachers.[26]

Though most teacher educators recognize the value of regular individual conferences with student teachers, time constraints typically limit their effectiveness. Because they cannot visit all their charges as often as they would wish, many field supervisors have come to depend upon the cooperating teacher as a provider of supervisory support, and to view their own primary responsibility as training cooperating teachers to offer the individual conference time needed by student teachers. These supervisors recognize that many cooperating teachers, though very successful as teachers of youngsters, have not been prepared to be trainers of teachers and may not have given thoughtful consideration to student teachers, their needs, and the variety of ways in which they learn their profession. In a clinical teacher education program based on the RITE framework, the value of individual intervention for stimulating analysis and reflection about methods and goals is communicated to cooperating teachers, as are the techniques by which such intervention might be accomplished.[27]

A fourth technique useful in promoting analytic and reflective capabilities in beginning teachers is the promotion of collegiality. Though it is clear that other professionals benefit considerably from substantive interaction with colleagues,[28] extended collegial interaction is not characteristic of teaching.[29] It is, however, central to the RITE model of clinical teacher education.[30]

Teacher educators in clinical teacher education programs modeled after the RITE framework systematically and consistently include programmatic components that encourage and even require student teachers to interact with and learn from their colleagues. Course assignments are made to groups as well as individuals; small-group program seminars offer settings for airing individual difficulties and seeking suggestions; and specific training is given in communication skills, classroom observation techniques, problem identification strategies, and use of conferences.[31] The thrust of including such components in the clinical teacher education program is to enable the students to use one another to promote analysis and reflection about teaching. Some teacher education programs have had success grouping their students into small cohort groups of no more than thirty and offering them specific training and opportunities to function as clinical supervisors. These students visit one another's classrooms, observe particular areas of interest or difficulty for the colleague student teacher, and offer feedback and raise questions about both teacher and pupil behavior. Colleague student teachers thus learn to offer each other many of the benefits usually derived from personal intervention by their supervisor or cooperating teacher, at considerably less expense in time to the program. Most importantly, they become comfortable with holding their own teaching as problematic, and thus with adopting an analytic and reflective stance toward their professional work.

Finally, a word about developmental concerns when promoting analysis and reflection. Korthagen observes that the approach to analysis and reflection must be gradual yet purposeful.[32] Reflective thinking should be a fundamental style of learning in students even before they enter field-based experiences, if they are to withstand socialization into established patterns of school practice. "The generally stressful period of the first field-based experiences, in which concerns about survival often play a central role, is very unsuited for learning to reflect on those experiences. Student teachers have to develop a reflective attitude *before* this period in order to become aware of the influence of utilitarian perspectives on their own activities in school."[33] Here again, though the RITE framework of clinical teacher education primarily focuses on living classrooms as the contexts within which to develop teaching capabilities, all components of the program, including those which precede field-based experiences, must be designed to support the program's goals. In this case, developmental concerns suggest early and consistent attention to the encouragement of reflective and analytic thought.

PRESERVICE CLINICAL TEACHER EDUCATION

The framework for clinical teacher education presented in this volume proposes to synthesize the research and development work of the RITE team with the products of a number of other researchers and practitioners in teacher education. This synthesis, when taken as a whole, presents a new and fruitful formulation of preservice teacher education that has the potential for substantially improving the preparation of the country's teachers.

The description of preservice clinical teacher education offered in the preceding pages has attempted to meet a purpose cast between two extremes. If this description had been too general, many readers would tend to respond with "We here at [enter an institution's name] do all this anyway," and then to conclude either that that institution's program was considerably more sophisticated than most in the nation, or that the RITE framework of clinical teacher education offered nothing new to the enterprise of educating teachers for the nation's schools. In these pages I have thus attempted to provide sufficient detail to allow the reader to discriminate between common practice currently pursued, and the potential for practice held by the RITE framework of clinical teacher education.

On the other hand, if the description in these pages had been too detailed, it would move the RITE framework from a set of concepts that give form to a program, to a list of specified prescriptions for implementation. This extreme would be equally inappropriate, for it would not recognize the diversity of settings and purposes across the nation's 1,200 teacher education institutions.

We hope instead that the characteristics of the RITE framework described and exemplified here will offer teacher educators a set of conceptual tools useful in examining purpose and method in their own programs, to the end of improving the process by which their students are educated.

3

Clinical Teacher Education:
The Induction Years

Hilda Borko

This chapter explores teacher induction practices and programs that are consistent with the RITE framework of clinical teacher education presented in Chapter 1. Its major purpose is to identify the essential features of clinical teacher education induction programs that help beginning teachers develop toward the ideal teacher described by Griffin.

In this chapter, the term "induction phase" refers to the first years of teaching, the years in which the teacher must make the transition from student teacher to full-status professional. This phase of a teacher's career (usually considered to encompass the first one to three years of teaching) has been given its own label in the literature on teaching and teacher education to signify that it has a character of its own, clearly distinct from both the preservice experience and subsequent years of membership in the profession.

It would not be unreasonable to say that the induction years mark the point at which a teacher begins in earnest to learn to teach. At best, the preservice experience can provide only practice in teaching. The first encounter with "real" teaching occurs when the beginning teacher steps into his or her own classroom. As Kohl suggests, "the essentials of learning to teach begin when one has the responsibility for a class or group of young people. At that point it begins to be possible to know what resources are needed, what questions need to be answered by more experienced teachers, and what skills one needs."[1]

The first year of teaching is especially important because of the significant impact it has on the development and character of a person's teaching career. In fact, McDonald, Feiman-Nemser, and others have argued that the first year is *the* critical year of teaching, determining whether a person will stay in the teaching profession and what type of teacher that person will become.[2] This view is illustrated in the following statement, which appeared in a request for proposals from the National Institute of Education:

> The conditions under which a person carries out the first year of teaching have a strong influence on the level of effectiveness which that teacher is able to achieve and sustain over the years, on the attitudes which govern teacher behavior over even a forty-year career, and indeed, on the decision whether or not to continue in the teaching profession.[3]

Given the unique character and importance of the induction years, particularly the first year of teaching, one might expect assistance programs for beginning teachers to be common in schools and school districts, but they are not. In fact, education stands out as one of the few professions in which the novice is expected to take on full responsibilities from the outset. And beginning teachers typically are left on their own to cope with these responsibilities — to work out their problems and define their roles. Most beginning teachers receive little or no help beyond what is available to all teachers in their district. Not surprisingly, when asked how they learned to teach, teachers over and over report that they have learned "on my own," "by trial and error," and that "it was sink or swim."[4]

Left to their own devices, beginning teachers are likely to focus on survival, on what is necessary to "keep the class under control" and "get the job done."[5] Their initial desires for assistance center on strategies and techniques that will help them accomplish these tasks. Unfortunately, these survival mechanisms may not be compatible with continued growth and development as teachers. As Feiman-Nemser suggests, a focus on "what works" in the short term (e.g., survival skills) may not be educative in the long run.[6] Concentration on survival skills may lead beginning teachers to explore only a narrow range of alternatives, and to develop the belief that good teaching is something you can figure out on your own, in a fairly brief amount of time. Furthermore, such a focus is unlikely to enhance their capacity to learn from teaching. Clearly, this pattern of development does not match the conception of the ideal teacher adopted in this book.

This chapter focuses on assistance strategies that will help beginning teachers develop toward the image of the ideal teacher adopted in this book, and that are consistent with the RITE framework of clinical teacher education. Most importantly, induction programs and practices considered in this chapter are designed to help beginning teachers become more reflective about their work and to foster in them a desire for continued growth and change. All programs and practices described are characterized by the seven critical features of clinical teacher education described in Chapter 1. That is, they are context-related, purposeful and articulated, participatory and collaborative, knowledge-based, ongoing, developmental, and analytic and reflective.

Many of the programs and practices described in this chapter were discussed by participants in the colloquium on the application of the RITE clinical teacher education framework to the teacher induction process. Participants in this colloquium were selected for their involvement and expertise in teacher induction programs. They began their task of identifying key features of a teacher induction program based on the RITE framework by describing what such a problem is *not*. For example, an orientation for beginning teachers designed to acquaint them with the school, personnel, rules, and procedures is not, in and of itself, RITE clinical teacher education. Assistance that focuses exclusively on helping beginning teachers to cope with the problems and traumas of their first year by providing survival skills and strategies is not RITE clinical teacher education. Furthermore, workshops or inservice sessions provided to all teachers who teach a particular grade level or subject area, regardless of their experience and skills, are not RITE clinical teacher education.

Participants in the colloquium also agreed that the assistance components of many state-mandated induction programs do not fit the RITE definition of clinical teacher education. Most state-mandated programs require that beginning teachers demonstrate competence in a standardized set of teaching behaviors in order to receive certification. Assistance is often viewed as remediation and limited to observed deficiencies in the generic teaching competencies assessed within the program. Because certification criteria must be consistent across the state, most programs are not context-responsive. Moreover, the primary function of state programs is gatekeeping or screening. Thus, competing concerns for individual teachers' professional growth on the one hand, and for establishing a defensible data base to support a recommendation against certification on the other, often shape the nature of assistance.[7] Given these missions and priorities, most state-mandated programs are missing one or more of the features that define the RITE framework of clinical teacher education.

Once they had established the parameters of RITE clinical teacher education, colloquium participants examined the induction programs with which they were familiar to see how well these programs fit. Not surprisingly, some of the programs were more consistent with the RITE framework than others. This chapter presents elements of several of these programs—as well as others described in the literature on teacher induction—that seem particularly compatible with the RITE conception of clinical teacher education and likely to foster beginning teachers' growth toward the ideal teacher.

Teacher induction programs may be viewed in terms of the four "commonplaces of teaching" described by Schwab.[8] For teaching to occur, someone (a *teacher*) must be teaching someone (a *student*) about something (a *curriculum*) at some place and point in time (a milieu or *context*). In the case of teacher induction, the *student* is obviously the beginning teacher. The *teachers* are the various people who provide assistance to the beginning teacher—experienced teachers, school-level administrators, district staff developers or supervisors, college personnel, and others. The *curriculum* includes the various forms of assistance provided to beginning teachers such as observations by and consultations with experienced teachers, observations of experienced teachers, meetings with other beginning teachers, and workshops or courses on specific topics. Given the RITE framework of clinical teacher education, the primary *context* is, of course, the beginning teacher's school and classroom. Secondary contexts might include teacher centers or local institutions of higher education. These four commonplaces of teaching are addressed in the four major sections of this chapter.

THE BEGINNING TEACHER

The student in the induction phase of a clinical teacher education program is the beginning teacher. The "typical" beginning teacher has recently graduated from a college or university preservice teacher education program and comes to the school without previous teaching experience. As Veenman points out, for this person the first year of teaching often represents not only an initiation into the profession but also an initiation into the world of adulthood.[9] This year marks the transition from the freedom of student life to the responsibities and restrictions of professional life.

Not all beginning teachers fit this description. More and more people enter the teaching force after involvement in another career or through alternative certification programs. For example, Sacks and Brady report that in their sample of 602 New York City first-year teachers in the spring of 1983, 56% had been involved in other careers prior to teaching.[10] In the state of New Jersey, college graduates with majors in subjects taught in the public schools may enter into teaching without courses in pedagogy and without a clinical field experience (e.g., student teaching). Furthermore, the projected shortage of teachers will create additional opportunities for candidates who have expertise in areas such as math or science, or specialities such as bilingual education, to be hired by school districts without having participated in traditional preservice teacher education programs.

Because of these alternative routes to the classroom and the diversity of preservice teacher education programs, people enter into teaching with vastly different pedagogical knowledge and classroom-related experience. Furthermore, given individual differences in learning styles, abilities, and backgrounds, even those who have completed the same or similar programs bring with them different sets of knowledge and skills. Finally, as Feiman-Nemser notes, prospective teachers enter into teaching with over 10,000 hours of exposure to teachers.[11] Through their experiences as students (their "apprenticeship of observation"), teachers learn teaching styles and techniques which they put into practice in their own classrooms. Clearly, then, there is great variability in the ranks of beginning teachers. As Griffin and Hukill comment, some beginning teachers fit the model of the undereducated, less-than-able, floundering newcomer.[12] Others bring to their first teaching assignment well-developed skills, precise sensibilities, and fresh ideas and practices.

Because of these differences in beginning teachers' backgrounds and competence, induction programs should be developmental in nature and responsive to the characteristics of each participant. Given this need for individualized, developmental programs, are there any similarities among beginning teachers that should inform guidelines for induction programs? Some prominent educators and teacher educators say yes. For example, Feiman-Nemser views learning as a central feature of teaching and sees all beginning teachers as students. She suggests that preservice preparation be oriented toward developing beginning competence and laying the foundation for teaching and learning. With the type of preparation she envisions, teachers would begin their careers with similar attitudes toward learning to teach, regardless of differences in experience and competence.[13]

While Feiman-Nemser proposes the development of shared attitudes among first-year teachers, other educational researchers describe actual similarities. Burden identifies seven characteristics, primarily limitations, common to most first-year or "first-stage" teachers:

1. limited knowledge of teaching activities,
2. limited knowledge about the teaching environment,
3. conformity to an image of the teacher as authority,
4. subject-centered approach to curriculum and teaching,
5. limited professional insights and perceptions,
6. feelings of uncertainty, confusion, and insecurity, and
7. unwillingness to try new teaching methods.[14]

McDonald describes the feelings that seem to characterize the induction or "transition" period as fear, anxiety, isolation, and loneliness. He also suggests that beginning teachers' problems or concerns develop over time. Classroom concerns first revolve around control of the whole class, and organizing and pacing instructional materials. Next, teachers begin to think about students and their individual characteristics as they relate to instruction. Finally, the focus shifts to the design and implementation of instructional programs.[15]

To respond to the limitations and concerns identified by Burden and

McDonald, as well as to foster the attitudes described by Feiman-Nemser, assistance must be specifically designed for the beginning teachers. What are reasonable goals for a teacher's growth and development during the induction year? Recall that in Chapter 1, Griffin presented this description of the ideal teacher:

> In summary, the ideal teacher is a knowledgeable, well-organized, and consistent classroom leader who interacts with students, colleagues, and patrons purposefully and effectively. This individual sees teaching as more than meeting with students, and works with peers on identifying and acting on problems at classroom and school levels of the system. The teacher values this opportunity to be integral school decision-maker, and others value the teacher's perceptions and knowledge about desirable practices. (p. 6)

Copeland argues in Chapter 2 that the development of such a teacher is an inappropriate goal for preservice teacher education programs. Similarly, it is unreasonable to expect a beginning teacher to achieve this ideal by the end of his or her first year of teaching. We can hope, however, that the teacher will make some progress from Burden's "first-stage" teacher toward Griffin's ideal. Specifically, it seems reasonable to expect that during their first year, new teachers will advance in both aspects of professional development identified by Copeland: basic capabilities, and aptitude for professional growth. Among basic capabilities, we can expect them to (1) increase their knowledge of subject matter, teaching activities, and teaching environments; (2) develop their abilities to diagnose student needs and to plan and implement instruction according to those needs; (3) develop positive working relationships with colleagues, administrators, and parents; and (4) become more secure in their roles as instructional leaders in the classroom. Beginning teachers should also emerge from their first year with a strengthened commitment to learn from teaching and an enlarged disposition to engage in exploration, experimentation, and change. To achieve these goals for beginning teachers' professional development requires an ongoing assistance program that is knowledge-based and stresses an analytic and reflective attitude toward teaching. Most importantly, the induction program must be sensitive to the context in which teaching takes place.

THE CONTEXT

The RITE framework of clinical teacher education defines the beginning teacher's school and classroom as the primary contexts of the induction program. As noted in Chapter 1, "The hallmark of a clinical teacher education program is its relation to the context in which it is carried forward. In contrast to general education and professional studies—typical components of teacher education—clinical teacher education takes place in living classrooms and schools. These real-life contexts and the people in them give form and substance to clinical teacher education" (p. 7). Griffin suggests that the relationship between teacher and context is a complex, mutually adaptive one. Within a program of clinical teacher education, this relationship provides "a means by which the teacher learns about, from, in, and how to act on the context." The following section focuses first on the kinds of contexts best for beginning teachers to "learn in" and "learn from," and second, on how clinical teacher education induction programs can help beginning teachers "learn about" and "learn how to act on" the context.

Learning In and From the Context

Perhaps the most important characteristic of schools within which clinical teacher education programs can flourish is that they support novice teachers' efforts to grow and learn. Feiman-Nemser provides several insights into the nature of schools that foster learning to teach. Rather than specific program characteristics, these schools have in common a *point of view* that acknowledges teachers as professionals and visibly supports their commitment to continued professional growth. Teachers in schools with this point of view consider their own learning, as well as student learning, part of their jobs. One finds two powerful norms in these schools. First, there is a "norm of collegiality," an expectation on the teachers' part that they will work together toward the improvement of their teaching. Second, there is a "norm of continuous improvement," an expectation that tools such as problem-solving, experimentation, and evaluation will be helpful to teachers engaged in professional development.[16] Although specific program features are not universal to "learning schools," certain activities are common. For example, teachers in these schools typically teach and learn from one another by talking about teaching, observing and evaluating each other's teaching, and interacting in ways that minimize barriers to communication. Clearly, schools with these norms and typical activities should be supportive of clinical teacher education induction programs.

However, Little warns that schools characterized by the norms of collegiality and continuous improvement, although well-suited to fostering continued development of experienced teachers, are not necessarily well-organized to assist beginning teachers.[17] Drawing on the experiences of several student teachers, she suggests that such schools may create a demanding, high-pressure situation for the novice. She goes on to say, however, that these schools, with their habits of teamwork and collaboration, appear capable of adapting quickly and systematically to better assist beginning teachers. A feature of the RITE clinical teacher education framework that may be missing from such schools is the norm of developmental appropriateness, which would ensure that programs are sensitive to the needs and concerns of novice, as well as experienced, faculty members.

Participants in a working conference sponsored by the RITE program on issues in teacher induction also identified three characteristics of schools that are likely to lessen their effectiveness as sites for induction programs.[18] First, beginning teachers are particularly susceptible to the loneliness and isolation that characterize the profession. To ensure their participation in the school community, attempts must be made to reduce their feelings of isolation. These attempts must be supportive and non-threatening: Beginning teachers must be made to feel that their requests for assistance will not be interpreted as signs of incompetence.

Another potential barrier to participation is the anecdotal pattern of communication characteristic of teachers with a shared history. Although these patterns are, to some extent, idiosyncratic to specific schools, they are based on a shared language of practice. Participants suggested that induction programs provide beginning teachers with the opportunity to become familiar with research findings, which form the basis of this language of practice.

A third school characteristic that could impede the progress of a beginning teacher in a program of clinical teacher education is the rigidity of the curriculum beginning teachers must use. For teachers to become analytic and reflective, they must be given some degree of autonomy with respect to curricular decisions.

Thus, beginning teachers can best learn in and from the contexts of schools that treat teachers as professionals, encourage and expect their continued growth and development, counter isolation by promoting communication and collegiality, and create an atmosphere of trust and support in which teachers are willing to share their problems as well as their success stories.

Learning About and How to Act On the Context

Beginning teachers must learn about their new educational community. They must become acquainted with personnel, services, procedures, and policies at the school and district levels. They must also learn about characteristics of the students in their classrooms, the parents of those students, and the community in which they live. Assistance provided within the induction program should help beginning teachers to learn about these contexts and to plan and implement instruction appropriate to them. Although such assistance does not, in itself, constitute clinical teacher education, it is an important component of a comprehensive induction program based on the RITE framework.

However, as noted in Chapter 2, teachers must do more than adapt to the context. They must also work toward its improvement. In fact, Griffin suggests that a good teacher will take a leadership role in efforts to improve classroom and school contexts. "This individual sees teaching as more than meeting with students, and works with peers on identifying and acting on problems at classroom and school levels of the system" (p. 6). Although most beginning teachers will not be ready to assume roles of leadership in school improvement, clinical teacher education induction programs should help them to work toward this goal. Thus, in addition to helping them learn about contexts, these programs should help them discern where in the curriculum they have flexibility and where they do not, which policies and procedures are "sacred" and which can be modified, and what strategies are most successful in working toward change within the system.

SUPPORT PERSONNEL

Within a clinical teacher education induction program, the role of teacher is filled by the person or persons who provide information, guidance, and assistance to the beginning teacher. The RITE framework of clinical teacher education does not specify a single right (or even best) configuration of support. Rather, it identifies some responsibilities of those charged with carrying out the goals of an induction program and suggests general characteristics of the person or persons who might appropriately fulfill these responsibilities. In this section, the responsibilities and characteristics of support personnel are discussed, possible staffing patterns for a clinical teacher education induction program are examined, and the issue of a nurturing institutional context for support personnel is explored.

From a review of operational and planned induction programs, we have identified three major areas of assistance to be provided by support personnel: introduction to the school and community (i.e., "learning about the context"), help with the procedural demands of teaching, and help with the pedagogical and substantive demands of teaching. For example, early in the school year, an orientation to available resource materials and personnel, the general curriculum and instructional programs used within the school, performance expectations for teachers, and administrative policies and procedures may help beginning teachers to feel at home in their new work environment. Throughout the year, they can benefit from guidance and expert advice in areas such as planning and implementation of instruction, classroom organization, management, and discipline, teaching methods and techniques, student evaluation and grading, holding conferences with parents, and other issues that arise as they enact the role of classroom teacher. These support requirements and various strategies for their provision are discussed more fully in the section on the curriculum of clinical teacher education induction programs.

A Plan for Assistance: The Colleague Teacher

In keeping with the essential features of the RITE framework of clinical teacher education, the assistance provided in these areas must be purposeful, ongoing, developmental, context-responsive, and determined collaboratively with the beginning teacher. One reasonable approach (although certainly not the only one) to designing a support program that meets these criteria is to assign primary responsibility for assistance throughout the induction year(s) to a person at the beginning teacher's school. Although this person would likely not be the sole provider of assistance, he or she would work with the beginning teacher to develop a support program that is coherent and tailored to the beginning teacher's needs and desires.

What are the precedents for assigning one person primary responsibility for a clinical teacher education induction program? Historically, support for beginning teachers has been in the form of informal "buddy systems," which have been in place in most school systems for decades.[19] Within such systems, the new teacher either is assigned or finds a more experienced teacher to act as a guide, confidant, and expert. Typically, there are no specific responsibilities or rewards attached to the role of "buddy teacher." Rather, the new teacher knows that he or she has a friend to come to with questions or concerns as they arise. Most often, buddy systems are effective in introducing the new teacher to the community, the school, and procedural requirements of the job. However, they are less successful in providing guidance on substantive and pedagogical issues.[20]

School systems that have implemented more formal induction programs also have typically designated a single person to serve as the primary support person for each new teacher.[21] The person serving in this role has been given a title such as colleague teacher, helping teacher, peer teacher, support teacher, teacher consultant, or mentor. In this chapter, I will refer to them as colleague teachers except when describing existing programs. The role of colleague teacher is more formal than that of a buddy teacher by virtue of formal selection and training procedures, specific responsibilities, and compensation for these responsibilities.

Selection of colleague teachers usually is based upon a set of specified criteria. Although the selection criteria of induction programs differ, the list developed by the Los Angeles Unified School District seems to be typical. In this district, mentor teachers must meet six criteria:

1. be a credentialed classroom teacher with permanent status;
2. have substantial recent classroom experience;
3. demonstrate effectiveness in classroom management, discipline, directed instruction, and communication with peers;
4. have performance ratings of satisfactory or above for the last three evaluations;
5. be willing to transfer to another location in order to provide instructional leadership and assistance in geographic regions with the greatest numbers of nonpermanent teachers; and
6. be willing to provide a designated period of service beginning with the date of appointment.

Other desirable characteristics of mentor teachers include a major or minor in the subjects taught; initiative and the ability to plan and organize; commitment to leadership role responsibilities; leadership or active participation in inservice training and staff development programs; personal qualities such as flexibility, patience, and sensitivity; positive professional relationships; ability to work well with students and peers; and several other experiential, professional, and personal qualities. The Los Angeles Unified School District also makes an attempt to match mentors and beginning teachers by subject area and grade level.

This list developed by the Los Angeles Unified School District is a good starting point for identifying the qualifications of a colleague teacher in a clinical teacher education induction program. We would expect a person with the demonstrated competence in working with students and peers, the subject matter expertise, and the leadership characteristics reflected in this list to be able to provide assistance that is knowledge-based and sensitive to the beginning teacher's developmental needs. A match by subject area or grade level as well as geographic region should help foster context-responsive support. However, the list of selection criteria for mentors in Los Angeles does not include problem-solving skills and the ability to be reflective and analytic about one's teaching. In an induction program based on the RITE framework of clinical teacher education, these characteristics are essential qualifications for a colleague teacher. In fact, in searching for a more complete list of qualifications, one finds that the ideal teacher described in Chapter 1 seems to have all the characteristics necessary to be an effective colleague teacher.

The important issue of the match between a beginning teacher and a colleague teacher, which is mentioned in Los Angeles Unified School District documents, has been addressed in other literature on teacher induction. Newberry found that extended interchanges between beginning and experienced teachers occurred only when the two individuals taught at the same grade level, and in nearby classrooms.[22] Preliminary analyses of data from the Model Teacher Induction Project support and extend these findings.[23] In that study of beginning teacher–support teacher teams in middle schools, two of the important criteria for the selection of support teachers were that the support teacher and beginning teacher teach the same grade level and subject area, and that they have classrooms in the same area of the school. Additionally, members of the more successful teams in that project had compatible ideologies about teaching, classroom management, and discipline.

Given the broad range of skills and knowledge desirable in a colleague teacher and the criteria for successful matching of colleague teachers to beginning teachers, it is likely that many experienced teachers with the potential to be effective in this role will be lacking in one or more of these areas. For example, as many school districts have noted in their plans for induction programs, being experienced and effective in working with students does not necessarily mean one has experience (much less expertise) in working with peers. These realities point to the importance of professional preparation for colleague teachers. Specific approaches to such preparation are discussed in the curriculum section of this chapter.

One additional aspect of the colleague teacher role deserves mention. Because colleague teachers assume responsibilities beyond their own teaching assignments, they should be given recognition and compensation commensurate with their role. Many school districts that utilize colleague teachers provide them with additional resources, primarily in the form of salary increments and release time. The mentor teacher program in Los Angeles, supported by state-level initiative, is particularly well-funded. Teachers selected as mentors receive an annual salary increment of $4,000. In addition, the school district receives $2,000 for each mentor teacher, allocated as follows: 23 substitute-teacher days, 70 replacement-teacher periods (secondary only), $350 mileage allocation, and $100 material allocation.

Other school districts have incorporated the colleague teacher role into career ladder programs. For example, the pilot Teacher Career Development Program in the Charlotte-Mecklenburg, North Carolina, school district has three levels of advancement following a probationary period of up to six years. As teachers achieve each higher level on the career ladder, they are given additional responsibilities and awarded a $2,000 salary increment. Assistance to beginning teachers is a responsibility assigned to teachers in the final probationary stage (career candidates) or at the first level of advancement (Career Level I).[24]

Using a model very different from the career ladder approach, several other school districts have looked to retired teachers as primary support personnel for beginning teachers. For example, in the Mentor Teacher Pilot Project developed collaboratively by the Bureau of Staff Development in New York City and the Barnard College of Education faculty, retired teachers assume the mentor role. During the program's initial year (1984–1985), 16 retired teachers were assigned to 43 new teachers. Mentors spend 12 hours with beginning teachers in September, February, and March, and 6 hours during the other months of the year. Their objectives are to help beginning teachers (1) develop their own teaching styles and confidence, (2) become decision-makers in their classrooms, (3) understand children's cognitive and affective needs, (4) become sensitive to different learning styles, and (5) broaden and deepen their repertoires of learning activities and effective ways of teaching and coping with the first year.[25] The Omaha, Nebraska, public schools presently are considering having retired teachers assist beginning teachers during the first month of the school year. Because retired teachers do not have their own classroom responsibilities, they may be ideally suited to provide ongoing support that is responsive to the particular needs of the beginning teacher, as those needs arise.

Other Models for Providing Assistance

In many cases, one person will be given primary responsibility for a beginning teacher's assistance program. However, other models are possible. For example, a teacher at the beginning teacher's school may be asked to work with a district-level specialist or supervisor to coordinate assistance activities. Or, at schools where teachers are organized into teams (e.g., by grade level in elementary schools, by subject matter in secondary schools), the entire team of which the beginning teacher is a member may work to organize the assistance program.

Another assistance model may be developed in school districts that operate teacher centers staffed by resource teachers or subject area specialists. Typically, personnel in these centers provide staff development activities for all teachers in the regions they serve. For example, the College of Education at the University of Maryland jointly sponsors Teacher Education Centers with several local school districts. These centers offer a range of preservice and inservice experiences including demonstrations, observations and conferences, and workshops for teachers and student teachers within the district. Two of the centers have recently expanded their programs to include seminars for beginning teachers. The Fairfax County school district in Virginia also operates teacher centers that are responsible for many of the district's inservice educational opportunities. It seems likely that, as districts such as these implement induction programs for beginning teachers, such programs will be operated through their teacher centers. Whatever organizational model is selected by a school district or individual school, it is crucial that the support personnel (individual or team) create a program that is purposeful, articulated, coherent, and responsive on an ongoing basis to the beginning teacher's needs.

Several induction programs also involve or plan to involve university personnel—for example, the Model Teacher Induction Project,[26] the Mentor Teacher Pilot Project,[27] and programs operated out of Maryland's Teacher Education Centers. Although the role of colleague teacher may not be appropriate for these individuals, several other possibilities exist. University personnel may be particularly well-suited to helping beginning teachers translate the knowledge, skills, and understandings learned in preservice preparation programs into strategies and techniques suited to their particular classrooms and schools. By asking analytic questions, university educators can help beginning teachers to look critically at their contexts and to discover new ways of being effective in them.

Thus, several different patterns of providing assistance to beginning teachers are possible within the RITE framework of clinical teacher education. The most common plan is one in which a colleague teacher assumes primary responsibility for the assistance program. In addition to demonstrating effectiveness in working with both children and adults, the colleague teacher ideally should teach in the same grade level or subject area as the beginning teacher, be located in a nearby classroom, and receive training and compensation for his or her additional responsibilities. Whether the colleague teacher model or another approach is selected, those who are to provide assistance must have the knowledge, skills, and resources to develop a program consistent with the features of RITE clinical teacher education.

THE CURRICULUM

Curriculum for the Beginning Teacher

The RITE framework of clinical teacher education does not prescribe either the content or the process (mode of delivery) of a program of assistance for beginning teachers. Rather, as it does for support personnel, the framework identifies characteristics essential to an induction curriculum. Specifically, the curriculum of assistance must be based on a beginning teacher's needs and interests as they arise during the induction year (developmental, ongoing), and must be appropriate to his or her particular professional situation (context-responsive). The beginning teacher must take an active role in identifying and selecting the issues to address and the time to address them (participatory and collaborative). In addition, the content of the assistance program must be knowledge-based. Finally, the curriculum (both content and process) must be designed to encourage the beginning teacher to be analytic and reflective about his or her teaching.

Although an assistance curriculum must be based on each teacher's particular needs and interests, one can identify several issues likely to be of concern to most beginning teachers. According to their self-reports, beginning teachers most often experience difficulty with classroom discipline, motivating students, dealing with individual differences, assessing students' work, relations with parents, organization of classwork, insufficient materials and supplies, dealing with problems of individual students, heavy teaching loads that result in insufficient preparation time, relations with colleagues, and planning of lessons and school.[28] The people responsible for planning assistance activities (e.g., colleague teachers) should be alerted to pay particular attention to these potential sources of difficulty and to consider possible ways of addressing these areas, such as those that follow.

Most beginning teachers have certain concerns that surface before the first day of instruction. Colleague teachers can be most helpful during this time by acquainting new teachers with the school and community, helping them to identify and locate materials and supplies they will need, and familiarizing them with administrative policies and procedures to which they need to conform. During the 1984–1985 school year, a colleague and I conducted a research project in which we studied in depth the professional development of two first-year teachers and factors that influenced their development. One of the teachers in the study reported going to the teacher next door (her "buddy teacher") countless times during her first days in the building with procedural questions and concerns. The other beginning teacher did not have similar support and reported feeling much more unsettled and ill-prepared than the first.[29]

Once the school year starts, many other issues will arise, particularly in the areas of planning and implementing instruction, and organizing and managing the classroom and students. As was discussed earlier, beginning teachers will probably initially want survival skills — strategies and techniques that will help them cope with the responsibilities and demands of the classroom. But survival skills may not be compatible with the RITE goals for clinical teacher education of encouraging beginning teachers to expand their knowledge through exploration and experimentation, and of strengthening their commitment to learn from teaching. One characteristic of successful assistance based on the RITE framework is that these two sets of priorities — survival and continued growth — are carefully balanced. Beginning teachers' immediate survival needs must be met. At the same time, they must be encouraged to approach classroom decisions from an analytic, problem-solving perspective, and to experiment with a variety of management and teaching strategies.

One method of providing assistance that balances these sets of priorities entails observations and follow-up conferences by the colleague teacher. By observing in the beginning teacher's classroom, the colleague teacher will be able to see any problems that exist and possible reasons for those problems. Conferences can then be used as occasions for helping the beginning teacher to reflect on the problems and explore possible solutions. Clinical supervision, although not the only strategy using observations and conferences, does fit the RITE framework of clinical teacher education. Cook's list of concepts and assumptions inherent in the clinical supervision model illustrates this fit:

1. a focus on the teacher's own goals;
2. the use of classroom data as a basis for analysis and discussion;
3. an "inquiry" or "problem-solving" approach including hypothesis generation and testing;
4. a commitment to a long-term program of growth and development, with a focus on teacher strengths;
5. an atmosphere of mutual respect and trust; and
6. awareness of the ultimate goal of improvement of student learning.[30]

In clinical supervision, the colleague teacher first meets with the beginning teacher to determine collaboratively the focus of the observation (e.g., student discipline, motivating students, use of instructional time). After observing, the colleague teacher analyzes data collected while in the classroom and then meets with the beginning teacher to discuss the observation. During this conference, the colleague teacher helps the beginning teacher to analyze his or her teaching by asking questions about what occured and why it occured. The colleague teacher also serves as a resource, drawing from a diverse knowledge base (theoretical, experiential, and research) to provide insights, information, and ideas for improvement.

Not all issues that arise in the induction year are best addressed through observation by a colleague teacher. For example, the beginning teacher's concerns about instructional planning and about student evaluation and grading can probably best be handled through discussion with the colleague teacher, subject matter specialist, or other support personnel. In the case of the colleague teacher, it may be possible to schedule a common planning period during which extended conversations or brief exchanges can easily take place. A teacher in our study reported that among the most valuable assistance provided by her "buddy teacher" was an explanation of the organizational structure of the basal reading program. This explanation, which occurred during their common planning period, enabled her to develop unit and yearly plans for her reading program.

Assistance with parent conferences can be provided by arranging for the beginning teacher to conduct several conferences jointly with an experienced teacher who works with the same student. In a departmental teaching situation, the experienced teacher might be a person who works with the student in another subject area. In a teaching situation where only one teacher is assigned to a class, a guidance counselor, reading specialist, or other special teacher may be appropriate. This strategy of holding joint conferences with parents proved to be very successful with one beginning teacher in our study. She conducted her first few conferences together with the math/science teacher who worked with the same child. The first-year teacher reported feeling much more confident in her interactions with parents following these initial conferences.

One of the most effective ways of introducing a new teacher to a variety of instructional and management strategies is to arrange observations in the classrooms of several exemplary experienced teachers in the building. Such observations, especially when followed by discussions of the observed strategies, can help the beginning teacher to expand his or her teaching repertoire. Another teacher in our study was experiencing difficulty organizing and managing a three-group reading program, since during student teaching she had dealt exclusively with a whole-group instructional format. Her principal arranged (in fact, suggested) a time for her to observe a colleague's reading program. The beginning teacher reported to us that results of the observation were immediate and dramatic: her own program improved overnight.

While much assistance to beginning teachers will be provided on an individual basis, for some issues it may make sense to offer workshops to a group of beginning teachers in the same school or school district. Workshops should be designed to ensure that beginning teachers take an active role, perhaps by allocating time during which they can use problem-solving skills to work on their own problems related to the workshop topic. A beginning teacher project conducted cooperatively by the University of Nebraska at Omaha and the Omaha Public Schools[31] can provide a model of workshops that accord with RITE clinical teacher education. The designers of this project offered a series of workshops at a centrally located public school focused on topics designated by participating teachers. During the second workshop, teachers were taught a problem-solving process. In small groups, they then applied this process to the problems with attention and listening they had encountered in their own classrooms. Each teacher presented his or her problem and, with the help of the small group, identified and evaluated possible solutions. In several of the subsequent workshops, the beginning teachers were presented with information and guidelines (i.e., a knowledge base) related to issues such as discipline and self-evaluation. They then divided into small groups and again used the problem-solving process to develop solutions to their own problems in these areas.

As the above discussion indicates, the curriculum for an induction program based on the RITE framework of clinical teacher education is likely to encompass a wide variety of issues and utilize a number of delivery methods. Because the program must be purposeful and articulated, some person or persons must assume responsibility for ensuring that all components fit into a coherent package, appropriate to the needs and interests of the beginning teacher. In many programs, this responsibility will be assumed collaboratively by each beginning teacher and his or her colleague teacher.

Curriculum for the Colleague Teacher

Because colleague teachers typically are selected for their ability to teach children, they are often less experienced in working with or teaching adults. For this reason, induction programs that include a colleague teacher component should, and typically do, provide professional preparation for those selected. Preparation for colleague teachers that is consistent with the RITE framework of clinical teacher education will have two major components: the content to address with beginning teachers (i.e., the knowledge base), and procedures or strategies for working with these teachers.

Content-oriented preparation. Persons selected to be colleague teachers may not be able to articulate the principles that guide their own teaching or the teaching of other effective teachers well enough to communicate them to beginning teachers when appropriate situations arise (e.g., during post-observation conferences or planning sessions). For this reason, preparation programs for colleague teachers should address the literature on effective teaching. Given the scope of this knowledge base, it will be necessary to select issues most relevant to the induction program and its participants. In making these selections, program leaders should keep in mind that colleague teachers must help new teachers to develop their own teaching styles and to become reflective problem-solvers in their own classrooms. In keeping with these priorities, programs for colleague teachers should broaden and deepen their knowledge of a variety of effective teaching models and techniques.

Several existing induction programs have incorporated content-oriented workshops for those in colleague teacher roles. For example, support teachers (and new teachers) participating in the Model Teacher Induction Project attended a research-based workshop on teaching effectiveness and classroom organization and management prior to the beginning of school, conducted by staff members from the Research and Development Center for Teacher Education at The University of Texas at Austin. Workshop topics included organizing a classroom, developing rules and procedures, holding students accountable for academic work, establishing consequences, and planning first-day activities.[32] Another examplary program, a 30-hour series of workshops for mentor teachers in the Los Angeles Unified School District, is somewhat broader in focus. Effective classrooms, cooperative learning models, and problem-solving skills and strategies are among the topics included in the program.

Workshops about research on effective teaching, teaching and learning styles, and the problem-solving process clearly are appropriate for colleague teachers participating in a RITE-based clinical teacher education induction program. Other topics that might be addressed in such a program include teacher planning, evaluation and grading of students, and instructional expertise in specific content areas.

Process-oriented preparation. Colleague teachers should also receive preparation in techniques for working with beginning teachers. Given the large number of resources available, each induction program will have to select the strategies best suited to its goals and objectives and the needs of its participants. In many situations, the preparation will include topics such as understanding the perspectives of beginning teachers, and observation and conference skills. For example, workshops for support teachers in the Model Teacher Induction Project focused on identifying and responding to the needs of new teachers. They included an overview of stages-of-concern theory, discussion of common concerns of beginning teachers, and instruction in diagnosing concerns and designing interventions based on those concerns.[33] Similarly, the State of California recommends that school districts participating in its mentor teacher program provide preparation for mentor teachers in the areas of adult learning theory, group leadership and facilitation, observations and conferences, modeling and demonstration, team building, and coaching.[34] Other possible topics for colleague teacher workshops include clinical supervision[35] and effective staff development practices.[36]

CONCLUSIONS

This chapter describes the common problems of beginning teachers and the practices designed to ease their entry into the teaching profession and to promote their continued growth and development. As we have seen, clinical teacher education plays a central role in induction programs—both existing and proposed— designed to help beginning teachers become analytic, reflective classroom and school leaders. The essential features that characterize the RITE framework of clinical teacher education—context-related, purposeful and articulated, participatory and collaborative, knowledge-based, ongoing, developmental, and analytic and reflective—characterize all four components of induction programs. They are prominent features of the goals for a beginning teacher's development, the contexts that facilitate learning to teach, the criteria for the selection of colleague teachers, and the curricula for beginning teachers and colleague teachers. The RITE framework of clinical teacher education can provide a powerful tool for the development and implementation of programs for beginning teachers.

4

Clinical Teacher Education and Professional Teacher Development

Beatrice A. Ward

The quality of the education provided to students of all ages is an enduring area of interest and concern in our society. Educators seek to provide, and parents and students seek opportunities to work and learn with, excellent professional teachers. However, individuals who are newly inducted into the world of teaching cannot yet be expected to possess all the capabilities of the ideal professional teacher outlined in Chapter 1.[1] To achieve such excellence calls for development, refinement, and expansion of teachers' knowledge and skills throughout their professional careers. The RITE framework of clinical teacher development is designed to promote this kind of career-long development of teachers.

This chapter will explore the clinical education of professional teachers from three perspectives. First, it will examine the characteristics of the ideal professional teacher which underlie the RITE framework of clinical teacher education. Second, it will identify commonalities between key features of professional teacher education based upon this framework and key characteristics of other effective approaches to experienced teacher development. Here, attention will be given to the ways the RITE framework extends and expands upon the strengths of existing effective professional teacher development efforts. The third section will consider issues that must be resolved at the school and school district levels if RITE clinical teacher education is to be a central component of professional teacher development.

THE IDEAL PROFESSIONAL TEACHER

The professional teacher has completed the preservice and induction stages of his or her teaching career, has mastered the basic skills of teaching, and consistently and effectively uses these basic skills to promote his or her students' learning. The roles and responsibilities assigned to a teacher with these sorts of capabilities have been defined in a variety of ways. Wise and his colleagues have suggested four views of the roles and responsibilities of the professional teacher — as labor, craft, profession, and art.[2]

According to this analysis, if teaching is considered *labor*, then the teacher is responsible only for implementing an instructional program in an already prescribed manner and for adhering to specific routines and procedures that are part of this program. The teacher makes few decisions and has little responsibility for the ways in which teaching and learning occur.

If viewed as a *craft*, then teaching consists of a repertoire of specialized techniques, developed by teachers over time and maintained because of their effectiveness in the classroom. Generalized rules for applying the techniques also exist. The teacher is responsible for following the generalized rules of application and for properly using the techniques.

When teaching is seen as a *profession*, the teacher is expected not only to develop a repertoire of specialized skills, but also to make judgments regarding when particular skills should be used without reference to prescribed routines or general rules of teaching. Professional teachers diagnose what is happening in their classrooms, consider potential solutions or improvements, select among these options, and study the effects thereof. Professional teachers summon theoretical knowledge, practical knowledge, and teaching skills in making such decisions.

The view of teaching as an *art* brings into focus its unpredictability. Teachers' use of theoretical and technical knowledge and skills is considered to be largely situation-specific. Teachers rely on insight and creativity as well as theoretical and technical capabilities to respond effectively to various contexts and instructional events.

What, then, is good teaching, and who is the ideal professional teacher? The concept that guides the application of the RITE framework incorporates the concepts of craft, profession, and art as central to effective teaching.

Although the ideal professional teacher might function as a laborer with prescribed duties for a short time, such as during the testing of a new curricular program or the implementation of a new teaching strategy, the restrictions of this view of teaching generally do not fit the RITE framework of clinical teacher education. The ideal professional teacher would continue to use prescribed routines and behaviors only if his or her observation and analysis in the specific classroom context led the teacher to conclude that students were learning successfully as a result.

A teacher at the professional level is expected to be expert in management of the complex social system in which classroom-based instruction takes place. The ideal professional teacher goes beyond this level of expertise. In addition to basic management skills, this teacher is capable of acting on the context to institute a variety of social systems. The teacher is cognizant of the subject matter concepts and the learning-to-learn skills students acquire while working within various systems. During a school year or even a school day, the ideal professional teacher may adapt the classroom instructional/social system to better fit the context in which teaching and learning take place or to provide students with multiple learning opportunities and experiences. Furthermore, this teacher successfully employs different types of instructional strategies in varying social systems with students of diverse ability levels and social and ethnic backgrounds, and whose learning needs vary.

The ideal professional teacher is a researcher and a risk-taker in the classroom. This teacher uses observation, analysis, and planning skills to study what occurs as he or she teaches and to design strategies, curriculum units, individual tutoring approaches, and other actions to improve instruction in his or her classroom. If observation suggests that a new approach is less effective than previous methods, the ideal teacher recognizes this state of affairs and acts to correct it.

The ideal professional teacher is knowledgeable and up-to-date in the subject matter that he or she teaches. In addition, this teacher is competent in the use of multiple approaches to teaching one or more content areas, and is conversant in what sorts of knowledge and skills students acquire when they are taught using the various approaches.

When secondary school students describe the ideal teacher, they draw a picture of someone who knows the subject area so well that he or she can re-explain things in several different ways to make sure all the students understand.[3] They stress that this teacher knows when a student is having difficulty learning, and meets and works with the student soon enough that the problem can be solved. Students mention the variety of instructional approaches the ideal teacher uses: "It's not just the same thing, done the same way, day after day." They say the ideal teacher tells students what the standards are for high-level performance in a class, applies those standards to all students, makes students work hard to achieve them, and helps all students who want to reach them to do so. "Everyone can earn an 'A', but not if you don't try. The teacher helps you [earn an 'A']." The ideal teacher also recognizes when a student has done well and lets the student know that he or she is pleased. Students say such a teacher "gives you a lot of encouragement, says 'you can do it,' and never puts you down."

Thus far, I have emphasized the instructional role of the ideal teacher. As prominent as this aspect of teaching is, the ideal professional teacher not only strives to become a master classroom teacher, but also engages in activities that extend beyond classroom-based instruction. The ideal teacher develops skills that will aid in the sharing of instructional expertise with other teachers. The ideal teacher seeks opportunities to serve as a mentor or master teacher who works with teachers at the preservice and induction stages of their careers to help them develop their instructional expertise.

The ideal professional teacher seeks opportunities to participate in research studies of teaching and learning and in curriculum development efforts that extend beyond what is taught in his or her own classroom. These might include research studies directed by a university professor, curriculum development directed by a central school district coordinator, or teacher training undertaken by a team comprising teachers and a teacher educator.

Particularly important for the ideal professional teacher is involvement in research, development, and training activities in which the teacher collaborates as a peer with researchers, teacher educators, and others in all phases of the work, such as the design, conduct, analysis, and report or product preparation.[4] Participation in design and analysis provides the teacher with new perspectives and new understandings of teaching and learning. The collegial interaction challenges and expands his or her thinking about instruction and about the role of a professional teacher. At the same time, researchers, teacher educators, and others capitalize upon the knowledge, skills, and insights regarding teaching and learning that the ideal professional teacher brings to a research and development endeavor.

The RITE framework supports development of the expertise and assumption of the roles and responsibilities characteristic of the ideal professional teacher. Nonetheless, as Griffin noted in Chapter 1, some of the skills, knowledge, insights, and understandings possessed by the ideal professional teacher may be acquired more efficiently and effectively through other training approaches. For instance, clinical study of teaching may not be the best way for a professional teacher to keep up-to-date in a subject matter area. Still, at the professional stage, many of these analytic, reflective, developmental, and collegial skills and roles are employed by the ideal teacher in the school and classroom context. Since clinical teacher education focuses upon what occurs in these contexts, much of the career-long education that will help a professional teacher develop towards the ideal teacher may be carried out within the RITE clinical teacher education framework.

THE RITE FRAMEWORK AND
OTHER EFFECTIVE APPROACHES TO
PROFESSIONAL TEACHER DEVELOPMENT

How would a program of career-long teacher development based on the RITE framework of clinical teacher education differ from other effective approaches to professional teacher education? In order to answer this question, participants in the RITE colloquium on the inservice level began by specifying the sorts of teacher education practices that would not be considered RITE clinical teacher education.

According to the colloquium participants, RITE clinical teacher education is *not* a single workshop or presentation, held in a central meeting place, that all teachers who teach a particular grade level or subject area are required to attend regardless of their skill and knowledge in the area(s) to be addressed by the training. Even if a training program extends over time, it is not RITE clinical teacher education if it is designed by a school-district, regional, or university staff developer based on his or her perception of what is needed to improve teaching with no input from experienced teachers and no differentiation based on the schools in which the participants teach. A teacher-developed inservice program built only upon practical knowledge is not RITE clinical teacher education. Nor is teacher development which treats all teachers as though they were undertaking their first year of professional teaching.

Although they found most of the professional teacher education currently underway in schools and school districts incompatible with RITE program requirements, the colloquium participants quickly pointed out some teacher development efforts that do match most of the requirements of the framework.[5] They noted that results of their own training efforts as well as data from research on effective teacher development indicate that training consistent with the RITE features is more apt than non-RITE programs to produce desired change in educational programs by effecting changes in a particular school, the culture of that school, and the excellence of the teachers who teach in that school.[6]

The similarities between the RITE framework and the characteristics of the effective teacher development efforts mentioned by the colloquium participants or reported in research on professional teacher development are explored further in the discussion that follows. As the reader will readily observe, in some instances, the key features of RITE clinical teacher education parallel those of other more effective approaches. In other areas, RITE clinical teacher education expands upon the strengths of existing programs, adding depth to the training requirements and placing greater responsibility upon teachers in areas such as analyzing, reflecting upon, and improving what occurs in their respective schools and classrooms. In a few areas, RITE clinical teacher education adds new requirements to current training efforts.

Nonetheless, taken together, RITE clinical teacher education and other effective approaches to professional teacher development have enough areas of commonality that implementation of RITE programs for professional teachers need not require a complete overhaul of the inservice teacher education system. Staff developers and others who wish to implement clinical teacher education based on the RITE framework have much upon which to build.

Context: The Defining Property of RITE Clinical Teacher Education

The defining property of the RITE clinical teacher education framework — that it is anchored in the school *context* — grows in importance at the professional stage of teacher development. Professional teachers are expected to be knowledgeable about the characteristics and complexities of the schools in which they teach and perhaps of various other schools. Their advancement as teachers requires improvement in the ways in which they conduct, analyze, reflect upon, and modify instruction in the contexts in which they work. Training that attends to and takes place in these contexts is more relevant and useful than training that does not.[7]

Various researchers have found that one factor that sets more effective teacher development efforts apart from less effective efforts is their attention to improvement of a specific school. More effective programs are targeted to improving the education offered to students. Thus, effective teacher development attends to the characteristics of the school and classroom in which a teacher teaches and in which students learn. Effective professional teacher development generally takes place at the school site.[8]

In those schools or school districts in which more effective teacher development efforts are underway, the already established emphasis upon context will facilitate introduction of RITE clinical teacher education. The setting in which teachers apply new knowledge and skills and the setting in which they engage in development activities generally are one and the same in these current programs and will continue to be so in RITE clinical teacher education. Both also recognize that there are occasions when it may be more effective to have training occur in one setting (e.g., a model or demonstration school) and application take place in another (e.g., the teacher's "home" school). In such situations, teacher development programs should consider the context of both settings.

Despite the commonalities, to meet the requirements of the RITE framework, the notion of context must be expanded in many current effective teacher development settings. RITE clinical teacher education moves beyond use of schools and classrooms merely as the places where professional teachers learn and apply new skills and knowledge. Attention is also given to analysis and interpretation of the information provided by those contexts and to improvement of contextual factors that may be inhibiting achievement of the desired excellence in teaching and learning.

Under the RITE framework, professional teachers study how and why things happen as they do in their own and other contexts. They explore what is required in order for teaching and learning theories and practices to work effectively in their own and other contexts. They investigate why a theory or practice works differently in one context compared with another. Teachers also learn to observe, analyze, and act upon different theories and practices as they put them into operation. They gain skill in assessing the extent to which a change in one teaching or learning practice achieves improved learning for students in a given context. They inquire into the aspects of schools and classrooms which facilitate or hinder such improvements. As a result, the area for improvement within a given context is expanded to include more than change in the teacher. Changes in curriculum, in school organization, and in the structure of the school day, for example, are also considered.

Thus, professional teacher development based on the RITE framework not only provides the required school-based environment for improvement, but also moves to inquiry into, analysis of, and action upon this context. It is these latter experiences which Levine suggests are necessary if professional teacher development is to stimulate basically skilled teachers to become excellent, and excellent teachers to remain in teaching positions.[9] Centering professional teacher development in the teaching-learning context, as more effective programs have shown, is important. Encouraging teachers to attend to and act upon this context, as RITE clinical teacher education demands, is even more essential if professional teachers are to develop towards the ideal teacher.

Key Features of RITE Clinical Teacher Education

Purposeful and articulated.   One of the key features of RITE clinical teacher education is a clearly delimited statement of the goals of teacher education and understanding of these goals on the part of all participants in a development effort. Based on their studies of more effective professional teacher development efforts, researchers generally have not identified statements of purpose and articulation of these statements to all participants as key characteristics of more effective programs.[10] However, two characteristics of more effective programs that have been identified suggest that the training that was conducted probably was based on clear, well-known statements of purpose. These are (1) an emphasis upon needs identified by teachers and administrators, and (2) the involvement of entire school faculties in the training effort.

For example, Rosenholtz noted that more effective inservice programs were "targeted at the needs teachers and administrators themselves defined."[11] In a study of effective teacher development programs, I found "school based needs defined by the teachers and administrators in the school drove the developmental efforts that were carried out."[12] Where teacher needs are the focus of a school improvement or teacher training effort, it follows that the same teachers who suggested the needs also will be knowledgeable about the goals to be accomplished.

Yet, it is relatively easy to envision situations in which selection of the needs on which teacher training is to focus and explication of the specific goals to be accomplished are not matters of general concern, input, or discussion across the entire group of teachers to be trained. Once initial suggestions are received from teachers, responsibility for selecting the needs to be targeted and for designing the training may be assigned to a small group that includes representative teachers, but not all teachers in the school. Less often, but occasionally, a staff developer or university professor from outside the school may be given the responsibility for needs selection and program design. In either situation, training goals may not be known or understood by all participants.

To some extent, adding the second characteristic found in more effective teacher development programs—involvement of all teachers and administrators in a school—increases the propensity for these programs to be purposeful and articulated. When *all* teachers and administrators identify and select the improvements to be achieved and all participate in the training, they should have a common understanding of the purposes of the effort.[13] Although situations undoubtedly exist where all faculty members participate yet hold different understandings and interpretations of the reasons for engagement in training, these circumstances do not appear in studies of more effective programs.

The RITE framework gives similar priority to teacher and administrator participation in selection of the training focus and the design of the training. However, the RITE framework does not require participation of an entire faculty as the primary vehicle for setting and articulating training goals.[14] Other reasons for teacher participation are more compelling (see discussion of participatory and collaborative feature). Rather, the importance of purposeful training and articulation of those purposes to all participants is compelling enough to warrant separate attention.

The issue of participation of an entire faculty brings to light another distinction between other more effective teacher development programs and RITE clinical teacher education. Much of the research that has been conducted regarding effective teacher development has focused on teacher development that occurred as a part of a larger school improvement effort.[15] Total faculty participation in such efforts would be considered essential in a RITE program as well as in other more effective programs. But the RITE framework also applies to other sorts of professional teacher development in which total faculty participation may not be necessary or appropriate.

For example, consider a training program in which a small group of teachers, within a school or from several schools, join together to build greater expertise in an instructional strategy appropriate for use only in a particular subject area or with students of a particular age. Such training might not be appropriate for all teachers in a school because they already possess the skills and knowledge, are not ready to utilize such complex approaches to instruction, or are not teaching that subject area or working with students of that age. Therefore, some teachers in a school might participate in this training while other teachers did not. Regardless, under the purposeful and articulated feature of a RITE program, the purposes of the training would be clear and would be understood by all the participating teachers. In addition, they would be shared with other teachers throughout the district.

Participatory and collaborative. The RITE framework of clinical teacher education calls for active involvement of professional teachers, along with researchers and teacher educators, in formulating, conducting, and advancing their own development. At first glance, it may appear that many effective teacher development programs already emphasize teacher participation and collaboration. In many of the more effective programs, teachers, administrators, and other professionals such as staff developers work together on collegial teams which identify needed improvements in the education program in a school and then set about designing teacher development efforts that support the implementation of these improvements.[16] Professional teachers in these programs provide input regarding aspects of the school and teaching that they think should be improved, and ideas about the steps to be taken to bring about these improvements. Teachers, administrators, and other professionals have a role in selection of the training focus and in conduct of the training itself.

To the extent that such collegiality goes beyond the offering of suggestions to involvement of professional teachers in observation and analysis of the state of affairs in their schools and classrooms, and exploration of the consequences of various actions that might be taken, these other programs may meet the requirements of the RITE framework for participation and collaboration. Even so, careful review of the responsibilities actually assigned to teachers is required in order to assure that teachers in fact engage in the inquiry, analysis, planning, and action called for by the RITE participatory and collaborative feature. The credence given to teacher input by other members of the collegial teams also warrants attention.

The RITE clinical teacher education framework views teachers as people to be worked *with* rather than as people to be worked *on*.[17] Teachers work as partners and peers with other teachers and with researchers and teacher educators from universities, central school district offices, and other agencies in the design, conduct, and evaluation of the training that occurs. A basic characteristic of their participation is acknowledgement on the part of the other collaborators that teachers possess skills, insights, and understandings that no one else can provide to a professional development effort. Their knowledge of the contexts in which teaching and learning take place and of what is required to improve these contexts is honored.

The professional teacher development that takes place when teachers participate and collaborate in this manner builds teachers' skills and advances their careers. For example, in a series of studies of teacher collaboration,[18] the participating teachers and the researchers who worked with them reported changes in the abilities and the career options of the teachers. The teachers gained skills in observing, analyzing, interpreting, and acting upon events that occurred in their own and others' classrooms and schools. They gained skill in understanding, interpreting, and applying information contained in research reports. They grew in their awareness and knowledge of the complexity of school- and classroom-based teaching and learning.

Several teachers also assumed new positions. Some became mentor or resource teachers who spend part of their time assisting other teachers in improvement of their teaching skills. Some are serving as lead teachers for district-wide staff development or curriculum development efforts. Some have undertaken graduate study in research, evaluation, and teacher education. In other words, proper implementation of the RITE framework's participatory and collaborative feature supports professional teachers in their growth towards the ideal teacher.

Knowledge-based. Professional teacher development efforts that are in accord with RITE clinical teacher education use what is known about effective teaching as the core from which program efforts build. Effective development programs often emphasize teaching skills that have been found to describe effective teachers in process-product research.[19] That is, they focus on teacher acquisition of skills that are utilized by teachers whose students perform better on some achievement measure (most often, a standardized achievement test) than comparable students in other teachers' classes.

However, the RITE framework does not stop with the process-product knowledge base. It calls for inclusion of knowledge obtained through practice, through development and study of theory, and through study of practice, as additional sources of information about effective teaching. Although the knowledge of external "experts" is employed throughout a RITE clinical teacher education program, the knowledge built through numerous years of classroom experience is considered as important as that derived from research and theory. Teachers' knowledge of procedures, strategies, materials, and processes that are more and less effective in instruction of various types of students in various school settings is valued and used.[20]

Working with whatever knowledge is appropriate and relevant to the skills and knowledge to be acquired and the context in which the participating teachers teach, RITE-based programs do more than merely present information about new teaching and learning theories, concepts, and skills to teachers. What occurs when a theory, concept, or idea is put into operation is considered, illustrated, and demonstrated. Teachers are required to apply the knowledge and skills in the classrooms in which they teach.

A teacher development program can introduce new skills and knowledge in a variety of ways. For example, teachers who already employ a theory, skill, or area of knowledge in their teaching may be observed, and the events and outcomes that occur may be analyzed and discussed. The observations may be done by other teachers or by an outside person such as a staff developer. Teachers participating in a development program may actually observe in teachers' regular classrooms, view videotaped episodes of teachers as they work with students, or listen to narrative descriptions of classroom events and discuss them with the person who conducted the observations. Assistance in analysis of such observations and in refinement of a teacher's use of a particular set of skills may be provided by another teacher who is more expert in that aspect of teaching, by a staff developer, or by some other "expert."[21]

Peer coaching is one approach whereby such experiences are provided to teachers in existing effective development programs.[22] Such programs have teachers jointly plan instructional activities in which new skills and knowledge will be applied. The teachers then observe one another as they carry out these activities. The performance of all teachers is reviewed by the participating teachers. This may involve two teachers working together, or the sharing of observations across an entire group of teachers. In their review, the teachers use observation notes, videotapes, coded information, and narrative reports. They note strengths of participating teachers and explore actions that might improve instruction. New activities are planned in which the teachers strive to improve their use of the new theory, skills, or knowledge. When at least one participating teacher is more skilled than the others, this teacher may conduct "model" lessons and provide exemplars for the teachers to employ as they introduce the new skills into their repertoires. A similar approach is to assign one teacher as the model (or coach) who observes and works with several other teachers.[23]

In reporting data from an effective professional teacher development effort in which they participated, Schlechty and his colleagues expressed concern about the models made available to teachers. In particular, they considered the individuals to whom teachers looked for information about and demonstration of new knowledge and skills. They noted that when a staff developer or other outside person, such as a university professor, assumes responsibility for presenting new theory, knowledge, or skills, participating professional teachers may question its effectiveness. If the new theory, knowledge, or skill can be demonstrated in the participating teachers' classrooms, they are likely to find it more believable and relevant. These researchers did not recommend reliance upon outside individuals as the sole source of models and exemplars in a professional development effort.[24]

Results of the RITE program's Changing Practice Study support the importance of demonstration of new theory, knowledge, and skills in teachers' classrooms. In this study, the professional teachers who were found to increase their teaching expertise significantly more than other teachers had worked with staff developers who focused on the teaching in the participating teachers' classrooms and who adapted their own behaviors and the presentation of information to take into account the contexts and needs of the professional teachers who were being trained. The participating professional teachers who gained in expertise had worked with experts from outside the school when the necessary knowledge and skill was lacking on site, but the expertise had been brought to and focused upon their particular settings. The models and exemplars were made relevant to the teachers' contexts.[25]

Neither the RITE framework nor other effective teacher development plans recommend that a professional teacher acquire new skills and knowledge solely through trial-and-error learning in his or her classroom. What is known about effective teaching — a knowledge base — should be made known to professional teachers. What *is* suggested by the RITE framework of clinical teacher education is that professional teachers test and refine whatever new skills and knowledge they acquire through application and study of them in use in their respective classrooms.

Ongoing. There are many aspects to the ongoing feature of RITE clinical teacher education. One is teacher participation in regular and frequent formal and informal discussions of ways to improve teaching and learning. Another is the provision of training that supports a teacher from the introduction of new knowledge or skills through their application and refinement in the classroom. A third consideration is for the logic and sequence of whatever training a professional teacher undertakes.

The RITE framework requires that clinical teacher education attend to all these aspects of ongoing teacher development. In contrast, most other effective teacher development efforts give concerted attention to the first two perspectives only. Few focus on the logic and sequence of teachers' training experiences across time. Emphasis is on the logic and sequence of the training in which teachers engage during a particular training activity. How well improvement efforts conducted during one school year fit with those from another is seldom taken into account. Even less attention is given to differences in training requirements for one teacher compared with another.

The importance of *all three* aspects of ongoing teacher development has been underlined in several discussions of professional teaching and professional teacher development. Possible explanations for what appears to be a relative lack of attention to the ongoing nature of professional teacher education have been posited as well.

For example, Levine found regular and frequent attention to improvement of teaching to be important to teachers' career development. She reports that in schools where teacher development was in the forefront of professional teachers' activities and where discussions about instructional improvement occurred regularly on a formal and informal basis, one found skilled professional teachers who remained in the teaching profession. Nevertheless, she also indicates that ongoing interaction about teaching is difficult to achieve within the cellular structure of schools. Teacher isolation is more typically the mode of operation than ongoing teacher sharing of information.[26]

The importance of providing support across multiple learning steps is underlined by Sprinthall and Thies-Sprinthall. They state that "without continuity during both the acquisition and the transfer phase, new instructional techniques may be placed quickly into desk drawers, atop new curriculum guides. As a result, both new techniques and new content quietly gather dust."[27]

Schlechty and associates call for development of experienced teachers to become "a long-term process rather than a short-term solution." They note that the success of the teacher development program they studied was attributable, in part, to focusing the effort on the improvement needs of individual teachers. They emphasize the importance of rewards for teacher growth over time. Having said this, they note that schools, and the bureaucracies in which they are embedded, are based more on a system of punishment for inadequacies than one of reward for growth. To illustrate, they point out that recent state and local actions to increase the quality of teachers have concentrated "on identifying and getting rid of bad teachers rather than on selecting and nurturing good teachers."[28]

The RITE framework of clinical teacher education calls for professional teacher development to become a regular part of schools' educational activities. It urges use of longer time lines so that comprehensive improvements can be initiated, applied, and verified; accommodation of differences in teachers so that each participating teacher has a growth experience; and incorporation of multiple patterns of teacher involvement so that teachers' expertise is utilized at the same time that new skills and knowledge are being acquired.[29]

Perhaps most importantly, the ongoing feature of the RITE framework calls for elimination of one-shot training events and of sameness across time in a teacher's training and in the teacher's form of involvement in teacher development activities.

Developmental. In addition to providing for the ongoing nature of teachers' professional growth, the RITE clinical teacher education framework takes into consideration teachers' career advancement. It calls for training professional teachers to assume new responsibilities such as peer coaching or curriculum development as well as for fostering increased excellence in instruction of children and youth. The developmental feature of the framework stresses this aspect of teachers' career-long growth.

Building a logical and sequential career development plan for teachers that extends across training activities has been advocated by numerous other researchers and teacher educators as well. For example, Howey recommends enhancement of teachers' careers through (1) creation of differential, realistic, and complementary roles for elementary teachers, and (2) development of more viable hierarchical leadership roles for teachers. He argues for professional teacher education that attends to what is known about how teachers learn and develop, how schools and classrooms affect teachers' learning and development, and how effective inservice teacher education is carried out.[30]

Given the growing interest in the professional careers of teachers,[31] it is interesting to note that most of the effective teacher development efforts that were studied during the early 1980s emphasized school improvement, increased teacher effectiveness, and increased student achievement. Implementation of a staged teacher career seldom was considered.[32]

On the other hand, the conduct of these efforts included several strategies of collaborative teacher development such as peer coaching, peer review, and use of resource teachers to provide models of and training in instructional strategies.[33] Experience gained in these programs, along with the positive outcomes of various teacher collaborations in research, have encouraged teacher educators, teachers, and others to recognize and use the strengths that more experienced and skilled teachers can bring to professional teacher development efforts. A few teacher development programs have been introduced that incorporate career development as an integral part of training efforts.[34]

One such approach was described by one of the participants in the RITE colloquium on inservice teacher education. The program described emphasizes both teacher effectiveness and differentiation in teachers' responsibilities across a teaching career. The program designers have developed a continuum of teacher skill, knowledge, and responsibility. This continuum incorporates knowledge and skills accumulated by teachers over time, knowledge and skills derived from research on effective teaching, and knowledge and skills obtained from research and practice in the area of curriculum development. A teacher's progress to more sophisticated understanding of instruction, more effective use of various teaching skills and strategies, and broader and more in-depth knowledge of subject-matter content and of the ways children learn this content, in turn, leads to responsibilities such as assisting other teachers in development of similar expertise and upgrading or redesigning curriculum guidelines and materials. Peer observation and peer coaching are used as tools for teacher growth and development.

Thus, this program builds upon a "more than" concept of a mentor or master teacher: That is, the teacher assumes responsibilities greater than or different from those of other teachers. And such a program also attends to the "better than" aspects of a master teacher: Teachers must progress to the upper range of the teaching skill/knowledge continuum in order to undertake broader responsibilities.

Some researchers have suggested the collaborative and participatory feature of effective professional teacher education may be difficult to maintain when a "better than" approach is taken.[35] Since the above program expects teachers with greater or more specialized skill and knowledge to assist other teachers in acquisition of similar expertise, it may avoid the conflicts which can occur when "better than" teachers receive increased recognition and compensation without a parallel increase in responsibilities.

At this point it is important to note that, despite the strengths of effective professional teacher development efforts, one characteristic of many of these programs may work against the developmental requirements of the RITE framework. This is the participation of an entire school faculty in a professional development program. As noted earlier, such programs often have the critical feature of an articulated purpose that is shared and understood by all participants. However, within a faculty, individual teachers may be expected to vary in their expertise and sophistication. All teachers should not be viewed as beginning teachers. Nor should they be viewed as equal in excellence. RITE clinical teacher education and a few of the more effective programs studied (such as the one described above) are designed to take advantage of these differences among teachers by capitalizing on the excellence of some to aid in building the excellence of others. But for some time into the future the vast majority of teachers, administrators, and other professionals who design and conduct teacher development programs probably will have had little, if any, experience with programs that take such teacher differences into account. Therefore, it is likely that they will be inclined to require all teachers in a school to engage in the same training activities. For this reason, in the near term, programs that involve a total school faculty may work against attention to teachers' developmental levels.

Hence, it appears that much remains to be done if professional teacher development programs are to meet the developmental requirements of the RITE framework. In particular, more programs need to recognize that there are stages in a teaching career and that the goals to be accomplished and the teacher development to be provided should accord with those stages and with the teachers who participate. Both within the training program itself, and in school districts, schools, and classrooms, professional teachers should be given assignments and responsibilities that change and become more complex, sophisticated, and diverse over time. As illustrated above, the basic structures of some of the more effective programs already attend to teachers' career development. What is required is more emphasis upon the developmental feature of RITE clinical teacher education in all experienced teacher training.

Analytic and reflective. By now it must be clear to the reader that the RITE framework emphasizes teacher development experiences that facilitate acquisition and use of analytic and reflective skills. In Chapter 1, Griffin points out that teaching is more than interaction with students—that teachers also plan, diagnose, evaluate, learn from experts, attend graduate school, and so on (p. 21). As he suggests, in order to conduct these aspects of teaching in an excellent manner, professional teachers must obtain information about what occurs in the classroom and school and, having done so, analyze and reflect upon this information to devise actions that will make what they do more effective.

In the RITE framework, these facets of teaching are central to the performance of the ideal professional teacher. Therefore, every aspect of a clinical teacher education program based on the RITE framework should engage professional teachers in examination of what is happening in their classrooms and schools, followed by review of their findings and action to improve what takes place. Opportunities to obtain and discuss new knowledge about teaching and learning, and to try out and assess the usefulness of this knowledge in the teachers' contexts, are an integral part of RITE training. Teachers, individually and collectively, are given time to obtain and analyze, and to reflect and act upon, data regarding the effectiveness of teaching, curriculum, and school-level support systems in their respective contexts.

Researchers such as Sprinthall and Thies-Sprinthall have pointed out the importance of such examination of real experience and of discussion and reflection about what is examined and how things might be improved. They argue for elimination of brief, episodic learning.[36] Cookbook approaches to training in which teachers learn a step-by-step teaching procedure and apply this procedure in any and all settings do not fit the sorts of experiences they see as promoting development of professional teachers.

Programs developed under either the RITE framework or the more effective program guidelines give more attention to analysis and reflection than the large-group lecture approach that to date has comprised much of the professional teacher development that takes place in schools and school districts.

Existing approaches to teacher development that *are* compatible with RITE clinical teacher education typically include such activities as self-instruction, peer study groups, in-class observation by peers and other professional educators, coaching by peers and other professional educators, individual or group collection and analysis of data regarding aspects of the education program, special discussion groups, and participation in university-based courses.[37] Several programs also incorporate data acquisition. Coaching and analysis of data regarding the education program, in particular, may include examination of what occurs, why it occurs, and ways in which behaviors and circumstances might be improved.

The more effective current programs that incorporate such development activities may require no more than allocation of additional time to these activities to meet the RITE requirements for analysis and reflection. Programs that include few, if any, analytic and reflective experiences obviously will require more extensive changes.

Summary

The characteristics of some of the more effective professional teacher development programs and the guiding property and key features of RITE clinical teacher education have many commonalities. Both types of programs focus on the context-related, participatory and collaborative, and ongoing aspects of teacher development.

To these common elements, the RITE framework adds three features that are currently given inadequate attention in most other effective professional teacher development programs. One is the requirement that programs have articulated purposes. A second is the call for teachers' training experiences to be developmental in terms of (1) a continuum of skill and knowledge acquisition, and (2) stages in the career of teaching. A third is the emphasis on the importance of an analytic and reflective approach to teacher development and to teaching itself.

Furthermore, the knowledge-based feature of RITE clinical teacher education expands on that of most existing effective programs, incorporating findings from a wide array of knowledge bases.

Two characteristics often found in some of the more effective programs are not addressed directly by the RITE framework. These are inclusion of an entire faculty in a training program and use of multiple training approaches. This is not to say that a clinical teacher education program based on the RITE framework necessarily excludes such elements. A RITE program may involve all the teachers in a school in a training effort and may use multiple strategies, but inclusion of these elements will be based on the goals of the program and the appropriateness of the elements to accomplishment of these goals.

Since much of the research on effective professional teacher development has looked at programs with a focus on total school improvement as well as on individual teacher improvement, total faculty participation in these programs was probably a purposeful match with training program goals. The same may be true of the inclusion of multiple training strategies. Use of the RITE framework, however, is not limited to programs of this nature. Hence, total faculty involvement and multiple training strategies may be appropriate in some, but not all, RITE clinical teacher education efforts, and then only if they take into consideration teachers' developmental differences.

In sum, the RITE framework for clinical teacher education provides an approach that supports development of the ideal professional teacher.[38] The next section of the chapter presents information regarding factors to be considered and changes that will be required if RITE clinical teacher education is to be used to this end.

IMPLEMENTING THE RITE FRAMEWORK IN PROFESSIONAL TEACHER DEVELOPMENT

The participants in the RITE colloquium devoted part of their time to consideration of problems that might be met were they to use the RITE clinical teacher education framework in the professional development efforts for which they were responsible. They also posed potential solutions to these problems. The discussion that follows builds from the issues that were raised.

Use of Knowledge

RITE clinical teacher education delimits the features that a *process* of professional teacher development should contain. It purposely does not prescribe the specific set of skills and knowledge a teacher is to acquire in a given development effort. Rather, it sets forth a description of the ideal professional teacher and uses this as the driving proposition in building a program that recognizes and tends to the complexities of teaching and the importance of the context in which teaching occurs. It accommodates and builds upon differences in the experience, expertise, and sophistication of the participating teachers. The RITE framework requires that the effort be planned and conducted in a certain manner.

Furthermore, RITE-based clinical teacher education programs approach the knowledge base somewhat differently than most other programs. Currently, other programs take what is known about a particular aspect of effective teaching and create training activities to help all teachers acquire those specified skills and knowledge. RITE programs consider the applicability of the research that was conducted and the knowledge that was obtained to the contexts in which teachers teach prior to initiating training based on that knowledge base. Teachers who already possess a given set of skills and knowledge engage in different development activities than those who do not.

Consider a clinical teacher education program focused upon teachers' classroom management skills, an aspect of teaching in which the knowledge base is extensive, and an area that has been emphasized in many recent professional teacher development efforts. In a RITE development program, information regarding participating teachers' present use of classroom management skills would be obtained. The assumptions under which various research studies on classroom management were conducted, and the contexts in which the research was carried out, would be reviewed. These would be used to evaluate the fit between the values underlying the research and those that prevailed in the teachers' schools and classrooms. Only when a knowledge base was judged to be relevant to their contexts would teachers, and possibly a staff developer or university professor, work together to undertake a development effort. Even then, teachers would employ information about their current use of classroom management skills and knowledge, and their own professional insights regarding day-to-day management of their instructional programs, along with the research knowledge base in the selection of training foci and content.

The colloquium participants suggested that this aspect of RITE clinical teacher education was a strength but, in terms of ease of implementation, also a weakness. Its strength resides in the applicability of the strategy to any situation and the soundness of the process that is required. Its weakness derives from the current environment for educational improvement. The attention of teachers, administrators, and school board members alike is just now upon development of the teaching skills that have been identified as exemplary of more effective teaching by research conducted during the past ten years or so. Asking board members to approve and teachers to participate in a teacher development effort that begins with analysis and reflection upon what is happening in their schools and classrooms, before listing the teaching and learning knowledge and skills to be the focus of a clinical teacher education effort, goes counter to this "basic skills" mind set.

Use of pilot efforts was recommended in order to demonstrate to the "non-believers" that a RITE clinical teacher education effort does, in fact, establish goals and objectives that further teacher effectiveness. Colloquium participants also suggested collection of data to substantiate that a program whose focus has been derived through analysis of current teacher strengths and review of the relevance of a particular research knowledge base to local contexts will promote as much, or more, teacher improvement than programs whose goals are set with no attention to such factors.

General Appeal

The premises from which RITE clinical teacher education builds and the key features of the strategy have high appeal for teachers, staff developers, and administrators. Terms such as "collegial" or "collaborative," "analytic" and "reflective," and "developmental" have appeared in the literature and jargon of teacher education for several years. As a result, many of those responsible for professional teacher development may assume their programs already contain the RITE clinical teacher education features when they do not.

In reality, few examples exist of teacher development programs that truly recognize and use the experience, insights, and expertise of teachers differentially. Few programs include teachers in decision-making regarding the focus, content, and processes of training during the early stages of program design. Even given the recent attention to recognition of teacher excellence and identification of master teachers, few programs differentiate training context, experiences, or roles for teachers with more experience or more expert teachers. Programs that are labeled "ongoing" actually extend for only a few months. And there are more discrepancies.

Participants in the colloquium suggested compilation of as many examples as possible of professional teacher development efforts that do meet most, if not all, of the RITE clinical teacher education requirements. They suggested that the contrast of extant programs with RITE clinical teacher education would help them and others understand what to look for when they move to introduce the RITE framework in their own teacher training efforts.

Role Changes

The RITE framework of clinical teacher education implies that the roles of several members of the school and school district bureaucracy will change. Teachers' responsibility for designing and conducting, as well as participating in, teacher development efforts will increase. Staff developers will be required to participate in collaborative, context-specific analyses and planning rather than offering prepackaged training efforts. School administrators will be expected to join analysis, planning, and training efforts and to find ways to provide the materials, time, and human resources that are required.

Such changes suggest that teachers, staff developers, and school administrators will require training in observation, feedback, and analysis skills, in working with groups, and in the key features of the framework prior to initiation of a RITE clinical teacher education effort.

Of the three groups involved—teachers, staff developers, and administrators—the colloquium participants indicated that acceptance of new teacher roles by district administrators, school board members, and organized teachers probably was the key requirement for successful implementation of RITE clinical teacher education. Such acceptance would give support to requests for resources such as release time for teachers. Without such resources, the colloquium members envisioned RITE clinical teacher education would be implemented only partially, as an add-on activity that would soon lose appeal even though it was effective and rewarding for teachers.

They further stated that the obvious relationship of the participatory and collaborative and the developmental features of RITE clinical teacher education to the master or mentor teacher role that is emerging throughout the nation gives added importance and urgency to the role-change requirements of the framework.

Mechanisms for Analysis

An undergirding premise of the RITE framework is that "real world" information regarding what occurs in a school and in teachers' classrooms serve as a basis for planning and promoting teacher development. The colloquium members noted that, to their knowledge, few mechanisms for obtaining such data have been developed and made available to school personnel. Without the addition of more and better means for looking at what is happening, they were concerned that, for all its good intents, RITE clinical teacher education would focus only on those aspects of teaching that are included in current packaged programs.

Individual vs. Group Growth

Given the recent emphasis upon people as groups working together to identify and solve problems in order to make schools more effective, staff developers and others may be concerned about the balance between individual professional teacher growth and school-level improvement when considering implementation of a RITE professional clinical teacher education program.

The RITE requirement that teachers contribute to as well as participate in a development effort fits with the collegial notion in other effective programs. A school faculty that has identified instructional areas that require improvement, in turn, is likely to include them as training goals in a RITE or any other program.

Assigning teachers with different expertise different responsibilities in a group effort will make a large improvement in most current teacher development programs. However, the colloquium members went on to point out that if we believe in continuing development for all teachers, schools' need for and use of expert teachers in training other teachers must be complemented by opportunities for those expert teachers to obtain new knowledge and skills and to engage in activities that expand their professional repertoires. They anticipated that excellent teachers who are part of a collaborative effort in which they serve as mentor or master teachers will begin to request such opportunities for individual growth. Hence, staff developers (whether district-, school-, or university-based) will be required to design procedures that respond to these requests independent of considering the needs of a particular school improvement effort.

The colloquium members further noted that professional teacher development may be included in several different educational improvement efforts within a school and a school district. A program patterned after the RITE clinical teacher education framework may not be appropriate for some purposes. Nonetheless, they recommended that the RITE framework should be kept in mind in all the training a teacher receives. Otherwise, one-shot, bits-and-pieces training will continue to be the norm. If this condition prevails, they feared that few teachers will have an opportunity to develop toward the ideal professional teacher.

CONCLUSION

The RITE framework for clinical education of professional teachers supports the development of a professional teacher who is knowledgeable about teaching and learning. It encourages development of a teacher who observes and analyzes what occurs in his or her classroom and who acts upon this information in order to improve what takes place. It furthers the progress of a professional teacher along a career path. It responds to the emerging interest in recognition of teacher excellence and the professionalization of teaching.

Since some more effective professional teacher development programs already incorporate some features of RITE clinical teacher education, introduction of the framework as a regular part of these programs will require expansion and extension rather than a complete overhaul of them. Such is not the case with more typical approaches to professional teacher education. Here, a new beginning is required.

Introduction of RITE clinical teacher education will require changes in the way professional teacher development is conceptualized. Based on the insights of practitioners currently responsible for experienced teacher development efforts, these changes not only are possible, but are urgently needed. To achieve them, all partners in the education endeavor — teachers, administrators, staff developers, university-based teacher educators, researchers, school board members, legislators, union leaders — need to grow in their views of professional teachers and of professional teaching in order to achieve the full benefits of the RITE framework.

5

Social and Ethical Dimensions of Reform in Teacher Education

Kenneth M. Zeichner

At the three colloquia (see Introduction) where we presented the RITE framework of clinical teacher education as described by Gary Griffin in the opening chapter, many people who are actively involved in the planning, implementation, evaluation, or administration of diverse clinical programs at the preservice, induction, and inservice levels offered their interpretations and reactions. Two things in particular stand out about the reactions and comments of these teacher education practitioners. First, despite several suggestions for the modification of Griffin's original formulation of the concept and its central dimensions — suggestions which are now in large part reflected in the opening chapter — there was almost unanimous endorsement of the vision that the RITE framework was proposing. Almost all of the practitioners strongly indicated by their comments and reactions that clinical teacher education based on the RITE conception was a desirable goal that should become an integral part of the reality of teacher education as soon as possible.

Along with this endorsement of the RITE concept of clinical teacher education, however, there was also a clear recognition that the implementation of this perspective will be a difficult and complex task because of the many conflicts between the institutional contexts of teacher education and the commitments that would be required for implementation of the RITE approach. The seminar participants offered numerous comments on how roles, role relationships, institutional arrangements, norms, and practices would need to be altered to enable RITE-based clinical teacher education to become a reality in their own institutions and others.

As a result of these meetings, I began to view the RITE framework as an *educational innovation* that will require substantial changes in the institutional contexts of higher education and primary and secondary education, and in the principles of authority, legitimacy, and control underlying them, if it is to be implemented in a manner that will foster the development of the ideal teacher described in the opening chapter.

Although the RITE concept and its central attributes are defined by Griffin at a fairly general level, and although the chapters by Borko, Copeland, and Ward demonstrate that there are alternative ways to realize the principles of RITE clinical teacher education in practice, there is a definite vision of the teacher and the school underlying the RITE concept which is at variance with what we know about the modal condition of the occupational group and about the school as a work environment for teachers. For example, in addition to a focus on the centrality of the teacher-pupil relationship and on pupil learning, the RITE framework is directed toward the preparation and continuing education of teachers who participate in making significant decisions about their work in the classroom and school. These ideal teachers are also learners who engage in serious reflection about the content and contexts of their work, both alone and with their colleagues, on a regular basis, and who "see" situations from multiple perspectives.

Almost all of the empirical evidence we now have about the social realities of teaching, about the school as a work environment, and about teacher education's role in facilitating learning about teaching indicates that these characteristics set as goals for the profession by the RITE framework are not currently evident on a wide scale.[1] On the contrary, the current condition of the occupation has led Lanier to conclude that in teaching, "opportunities to exercise informed judgment, engage in thoughtful discourse, and participate in reflective decision-making are practically nonexistent."[2]

Numerous analyses, conducted from a variety of ideological and political perspectives, have concluded that the effect of many of the recent policies affecting teachers has been to promote greater external control over the content, processes, and outcomes of teachers' work and to encourage teachers to adopt conformist orientations to self and society as well as technical orientations to the role of teacher.[3] Although it is clear that many teachers do not passively carry out the directives contained in these technically-oriented reforms,[4] it is also clear that most schools do not actively encourage teachers to engage in the kinds of practices the RITE framework advocates.

Because the implementation of RITE-based clinical teacher education would necessarily entail a host of complex and demanding changes in the assumptions, norms, and structures underlying modal practice, the danger arises that the RITE framework will be implemented in ways that would serve to reinforce existing patterns of conduct that are essentially in conflict with its goals. This irony of educational reform has occurred many times before and can easily happen once again if in the implementation of RITE-based clinical teacher education we do not give explicit attention to the social and ethical dimensions of reform.

This chapter will consider various aspects of the problem of implementing clinical teacher education within organizational contexts that are generally unsupportive of the underlying goals of the approach. First, I will examine the literature on other educational innovations to see what can be learned about the social and institutional factors that influence the implementation of an innovation. Particular attention will be given to a recent evaluation of the program of Individually Guided Education (IGE) conducted by the Wisconsin Center for Education Research. Second, I will examine the current institutional contexts of clinical teacher education to identify the major institutional dimensions that need to be addressed in the implementation of the RITE framework. I will then examine the concept of clinical teacher education in relation to two different conceptions of the teacher's role: (1) the teacher as a professional decision-maker, and (2) the teacher as a skilled craftsperson. Two of the critical attributes of the RITE framework will be explored to demonstrate how they can be realized in ways that reflect different ethical commitments. Finally, specific suggestions will be offered for how the contexts of teacher education and schooling will need to be confronted in order to realize the ethical commitments in the RITE framework to the intellectual and practical empowerment of teachers.

In arguing against implementation of the RITE framework of clinical teacher education such that it becomes merely a symbolic process that in the final analysis lends credibility to the very practices and values it seeks to change, we are not implying support for what Fullan and Pomfret refer to as the "fidelity perspective" of implementation. Here the concern is with having the implementation of the program conform closely to a specific set of behavioral criteria formulated by program designers. In such designs there is little or no provision for the adaptation of the innovation to specific contexts or for the improvement or elaboration of the conception by users.[5] On the contrary, we recognize and support the need for alternative models of clinical teacher education in practice and for what Fullan and Pomfret call a "mutual adaptation" perspective on implementation. Griffin has clearly presented the RITE framework in such a way as to encourage initiative in adaptation. The problem arises when the adaptation to local conditions goes so far as to undermine the ethical basis of the original conception. It is with this critical problem that this chapter is concerned.

THE SOCIAL DIMENSIONS OF IMPLEMENTING EDUCATIONAL INNOVATIONS

Griffin has concluded it is now axiomatic that the settings in which teachers and others are expected to change their behavior influence the success of the efforts toward change.[6] Almost without exception, the empirical literature on the implementation of educational innovations supports Griffin's conclusions regarding the transformation of innovations by the social conditions in which they are realized, and points to the importance of viewing the process of implementation within an institutional context. Fullan and Pomfret conclude that the problem has not been in getting people to try an innovation or even to see an innovation in certain ways. On the contrary, Fullan and Pomfret argue, "the main problem appears to be that curriculum change necessitates certain organizational changes, particularly changes in the roles and role relationships of those organizational members most directly involved in putting the innovation into practice."[7] These organizational changes required for the implementation of an innovation are difficult to accomplish because of the coercive power of the reification of social reality, a result of the process of institutionalization. According to Berger and Luchmann, "institutions by the very fact of their existence control human conduct by setting up predefined patterns of conduct, which channel it in one direction as against the many other directions which would theoretically be possible."[8] Although this objectification of everyday reality is not totally coercive (i.e., relations between individuals and the social world remain dialectical in character), deviations from institutionally sanctioned regularities become difficult to accomplish because the existing structure serves as a barrier to recognition and experimentation with alternatives.[9]

Drawing upon the work of Berger and Luchmann on the social construction of institutional reality, Popkewitz argues that "schooling is a socially constructed endeavor. To participate in the world of schooling is to participate in a social world which maintains particularities of reasoning, actions, and values."[10] According to this point of view, schooling and teacher education have both surface and underlying layers of meaning.[11] The underlying layer of institutional meaning consists of assumptions, predispositions, and values (e.g., about knowledge, learning, and work) which give plausibility and legitimacy to organizational structures and manifest actions. The history of the implementation of educational innovations has shown the tremendous resilience of this "deep structure" of institutions in the face of innovations despite their often willing adoption, frequent changes in surface patterns of conduct, and the possession by users of the knowledge and skills necessary to implement the innovations behaviorally.[12]

One consequence of the coercive power of this deeper structure of institutional reality is the tremendous variation in the implementation of educational innovations in different organizational contexts. For example, Fullan and Pomfret, in one of the most comprehensive analyses to date, conclude that "there are definite variations in the degree to which the same innovation is implemented by different individuals and organizations and the degree to which some components of an implementation are implemented more effectively than others."[13] Similarly, Parlett and Hamilton have concluded that an instructional system (or idealized conception of an innovation),

> when adopted, undergoes modifications that are rarely trivial. The instructional system may remain as a shared idea, abstract model, slogan, or shorthand, but it assumes a different form in every situation. Its constituent elements are emphasized or deemphasized, expanded or truncated, as teachers, administrators, technicians, and students interpret and reinterpret the instructional system for their particular setting. In practice, objectives are commonly reordered, redefined, abandoned, or forgotten. The original "ideal" formulation ceases to be accurate or indeed of much relevance.[14]

Significantly, these modifications of educational innovations within different organizational contexts seem ultimately to legitimate and reinforce the underlying layer of meaning or deep structure of an institution. Innovations are most often incorporated into existing patterns of behavior and belief that sustain current arrangements, and ironically are often used to justify the very institutional characteristics the reform was intended to challenge.[15] Research has clearly shown that unless the implementation of an educational innovation directly confronts the underlying patterns of belief, values, and norms that sustain current institutional arrangements, we will be left with the familiar pattern of change but no change.

A recent evaluation of the program of Individually Guided Education (IGE) conducted by the Wisconsin Center for Education Research illustrates this process with regard to an organizational innovation that was in use in nearly 3,000 North American elementary schools in 1975.[16] Developed in the late 1960s and early 1970s at the Wisconsin Research and Development Center, IGE was intended as a practical means of meeting the individual learning needs of diverse pupils in elementary schools. This system proposed many specific changes in conventional patterns of school administration, instructional methods, and organizational arrangements.[17] For example, a key element in the program was the frequent regrouping of children according to data provided by assessment of their learning needs, which was a significant change from the traditional pattern of age-graded classes.

In 1976, the Wisconsin Center began a multiphased evaluation of the impact of IGE on elementary schools. This comprehensive evaluation found that, generally, the degree of implementation of IGE was very low. According to Romberg, nearly 60% of the sample of 900 schools could at best be called nominal adopters of IGE, and only about 20% could be called ture implementers.[18] A key finding of the second phase of the evaluation was the variation between schools in IGE implementation, which reflected differential understanding of the IGE components, which in turn reflected different assumptions, values, and norms about teaching, learning, and schooling that sustained the organizational realities of each school.

Importantly, in most schools this low degree of implementation reflected a lack of understanding of or agreement with the goals of IGE as conceived by program designers. The IGE procedures were used in most schools for other ends.

> Schools did not merely adapt the [IGE] program, making modifications to reach the same goal; rather, they revised both the technology and its espoused goals. Such revisions helped to conserve quite different institutional conditions—in each of the schools a different style of work, conception of knowledge, and professional ideology was maintained.[19]

Popkewitz, Tabachnick, and Wehlage identified three institutional patterns of IGE implementation in their sample, which they termed *technical, constructive,* and *illusory.* Different assumptions about teaching, learning, and schooling in the three types of schools determined the form that IGE took in those schools. For example, in schools with illusory IGE programs, the label of IGE was used symbolically to justify the maintenance of current arrangements. In other schools, the goal became to increase the efficiency of current practices (technical implementation) or to accomplish different goals (constructive implementation). The basic changes in the traditional classroom structure and in instructional practices hoped for by the IGE designers did not occur in most schools.[20] Teachers and principals in the six schools translated key IGE concepts such as "individualization" to correspond to certain beliefs they already held about children and learning and, as a consequence, conserved existing pedagogical relationships rather than changing them. The old conditions were given a new source of credibility and reasonableness through the symbolic form and practices of the reform itself.[21] Popkewitz, Tabachnick, and Wehlage caution would-be reformers:

> Those who would introduce educational reform measures must recognize that their intentions, goals, and technologies are profoundly subject to the specific dynamics affecting a particular institution. Reformers should expect that their programs will be interpreted, modified, and used in accordance with the professional ideologies which are asserted through institutions as well as in response to conditions outside of institutions.[22]

The history of reform in teacher education reveals many parallels with the implementation of other reforms in education and with the IGE example just described. For over fifty years, teacher education has been the focus of reports and proposals for reform at all levels.[23] Despite these initiatives for reform both from within and from outside the field, nearly all agree their influence has been meager on the course of teacher education and on the inability of teacher education programs to engineer systematic and comprehensive changes.[24] The implementation of reform in teacher education, like reform in education generally, has frequently been piecemeal in character, addressing only isolated parts of complex and interrelated social systems,[25] and has frequently focused on changes in the surface characteristics of programs (e.g., increasing the number of clock hours spent in clinical experiences) while ignoring the underlying values, role relationships, and institutional structures that sustain the very practices that are the targets of initiatives for change. This has been the case despite the fact that many of the reform proposals themselves have addressed the institutional dimensions of reform, and despite the often enthusiastic adoption of some components of reform proposals.

Despite expressed interest in field-based teacher education programs over the past few years and the encouragement of reformers, an accurate description of current practice paints a picture very familiar to any who have had contact with teacher education over the past 25 years. The student teaching program is generally a low cost, expedient instructional effort.[26]

Fullan and Pomfret identify five dimensions of the implementation of curricular innovations. Although their analysis does not give explicit attention to the problem of reform in teacher education, this framework together with their notions of the "determinants of implementation" can serve as useful heuristics for examining the social and ethical dimensions of reform in teacher education. According to Fullan and Pomfret, the implementation of educational innovations requires attention to the following issues:

1. subject matter and/or materials (curricular substance);
2. roles and role relationships;
3. organizational structures (i.e., the conditions under which users interact);
4. the knowledge and understanding that users have of an innovation and its various components (e.g., the philosophy, values, assumptions);
5. users' valuing of and commitment to the specific components of an innovation and its ethical basis.

Fullan and Pomfret go on to argue that the successful implementation of an innovation (i.e., its ability to influence curricular substance, role relationships, etc.) is affected by the characteristics of the innovation itself (e.g., its explicitness and complexity), the strategies used to introduce and implement the innovation (e.g., staff development, resource support), the characteristics of the institutions in which the innovation is to be implemented (e.g., environmental support), and the characteristics of macro-sociopolitical factors outside of the institutions in which the innovation is to be implemented (e.g., policies of political agencies outside of the adopting organizations).[28]

THE INSTITUTIONAL CONTEXTS OF
CLINICAL TEACHER EDUCATION

Several recent analyses of the institutional contexts of teacher education, especially at the preservice and inservice levels, vividly document the current conditions and policies in institutions of higher education, schools, and professional organizations that are likely to inhibit the implementation of the RITE reform proposal.[29]

Low Status and Low Prestige

First, in addition to acknowledging the well-known low status of teacher education in institutions of higher education,[30] it is important to recognize status distinctions *within* teacher education that are relevant to the issue of reform in the clinical component of teacher education. Specifically, status within preservice teacher education seems to be inversely correlated with proximity to the field.[31] Those who conduct clinical teacher education at the preservice level (cooperating teachers, university supervisors) are often those with the least status and formal power within schools and colleges of education—those least likely to be able to effect the kinds of changes in the roles, role relationships, organizational structures, and underlying culture of the clinical component of teacher education that are necessary for realization of the critical features of the RITE approach. Note, for example, the common practice of employing graduate students and junior faculty to supervise in clinical programs, the minimal standards for the selection of cooperating teachers and the token payments given to these clinical educators for their work, and the lack of attention in most institutions to the preparation of both cooperating teachers and university supervisors for their roles.[32]

The problem of low status and low prestige is evident at the inservice level as well. Moore and Hyde, for example, have observed that those who conduct staff development are located fairly low in the bureaucratic hierarchy of school systems and are typically isolated from major reform initiatives in curriculum and instruction.[33] As Schlechty and Crowell point out, "Those who run staff development seldom run schools."[34] Staff development is typically conducted on a part-time basis by those who have other major responsibilities, and as Lanier points out, it "offers few career rewards to those who emerge as its leaders."[35] Finally, as in preservice clinical teacher education, there is almost no attention given to the training of staff developers for their roles either by colleges and universities or by school systems.[36] The very newness of attention to roles for clinical teacher educators who would work with beginning teachers (e.g., mentors, colleague

teachers) is sufficient evidence of the traditionally low priority given to induction in school systems across the United States.[37]

Little Investment of Resources

One consequence of the low status of those who conduct clinical teacher
education is the low investment of resources (both financial and human) in
the maintenance and improvement of the enterprise. For example, the well-
known studies by Peseau and Orr of funding patterns in 63 institutions of
higher education clearly document the "outrageous underfunding of teacher
education" at the preservice level.[38] Peseau concluded, for instance, that the
average direct cost of instruction per year for the preparation of an
undergraduate student in teacher education was only 50% as much as the
average spent to educate undergraduates in all university disciplines.[39]

Various explanations have been offered for this meager financial investment in teacher education. Some have criticized state funding formulas and
internal college or university policies that place teacher education programs
with other undergraduate programs of low complexity (i.e., those without
clinical components).[40] Others have claimed the limited allocation of funds
reflects traditions and characteristics of the larger society and university community, such as the politically weak status of the occupational group and its
clients (women and children) and the allegedly weak and questionable
knowledge base for teacher education. Although there is much debate over
the causes of current funding patterns,[41] there is little dispute that the common rhetoric regarding the importance of teacher education in higher education is rarely supported in practice by the commitment of financial resources
which would reflect that importance.

The picture of investment of financial resources at the inservice level is
very different from that at the preservice level. Here, there appears to be
more financial commitment than has been thought, with the exception of the
traditionally low investment in induction activities for beginning teachers.
For example, Howey and Vaughan report that the magnitude of staff
development has typically been underestimated because many expenditures
attributable to staff development, ranging from $1,000 to $1,760 per teacher
per year, have not been recognized as staff development costs by school
districts.[42] In Moore and Hyde's study, actual staff development costs were
fifty to sixty times district estimates.[43] A recent national survey of staff development practices estimated that in each district there is one person with
some staff development responsibility available for approximately every
seven teachers.[44]

Although there seems to be no lack of resources with which to address
the staff development needs of teachers, teachers typically report that they
participate in relatively little staff development during the school year. For
example, in the national survey of staff development cited above, the great
majority of teachers reported that they engaged in some form of staff

development not more than once a year.[45] Here the problem is due not to a lack of resources, but to the underutilization of the resources available. Among the many reasons for this underutilization of resources, the most important is the lack of coordination of staff development activities. The fragmented and diffuse nature of staff development will be discussed below.

A second aspect of this low investment of resources is the meager allocation of human resources and the lack of personal commitment of staff to the clinical education of teachers. Clark and Marker highlight a fact that has typically been ignored in proposals to reform teacher education—that prospective teachers (elementary or secondary) generally spend the majority of their time during preservice teacher education with faculty outside of schools and colleges of education, for whom teacher education is clearly a peripheral concern.[46]

Furthermore, as Lanier points out, even within schools and colleges of education, only a small portion of faculty are involved more than tangentially in teacher education programs, and fewer still are identified with and rewarded for their specific contributions to teacher education.[47] Judge has noted the common tendency for education faculty to distance themselves from teacher education.[48] There is a common tendency (even for faculty who are assigned formal program responsibilities) to identify with a specific disciplinary area and not with the task of educating teachers.[49]

> Identifying primarily with their disciplines, the professors teaching foundations courses to prospective teachers (e.g., the psychology, sociology, history, or philosophy of education) tend to deny their teacher education role and identify those who teach methods courses and supervise practice teaching as the real teacher educators. But most professors of teaching methods courses would disagree. Identifying with the school subjects of their expertise, they tend to consider themselves science educators, mathematics educators, or reading educators and point to those who coordinate and supervise student teachers as the real teacher educators. Those who supervise fieldwork in the schools are probably the only faculty, as a group, who publicly identify themselves as teacher educators.[50]

This lack of faculty commitment to undergraduate teacher preparation is understandable given the reference groups and reward systems for educational faculty and staff. There is little doubt that the clinical education of teachers stands at the very bottom of the status hierarchy within schools and colleges of education. Despite all of the talk about an "all-university approach" to teacher education and about linkages between the clinical component and other aspects of teacher preparation, the only personnel who spend significant time on clinical teacher education are the graduate students, junior faculty, and cooperating teachers who supervise students, and the academic staff who administer programs and supporting services. Even for most of those who supervise, the clinical education of teachers is often a function secondary to the major priorities of teaching children, continuing graduate studies, and conducting research, and understandably so, since, as Clark and Marker point out, university reward systems pay little attention to time spent in "road running."[51]

The picture at the inservice level is very similar to that for the clinical education of prospective teachers. Although there seems to be no lack of school district personnel in staff development activities, many if not most of these personnel engage in staff development only on a part-time basis and only as an activity secondary to carrying out primary responsibilities.[52] Hutson has concluded that staff development remains everyone's issue but no one's priority.[53] The little formal supervision that is provided to teachers has generally been more evaluative — more concerned with assessment — than nurturant of teachers' continuing professional development.[54] Teachers appear to obtain most of their assistance from outside of the formal mechanisms for both staff development and supervision, from informal interactions with other teachers. This informal teacher-teacher assistance predominates despite the assignment of significant human resources to formal staff development and despite the fact that teachers on the whole do not visit each other or observe each other frequently.[55]

Fragmented, Uncoordinated, and Isolated

A third characteristic of teacher education that is relevant for the reform of the clinical education of teachers is its highly fragmented nature, the isolation of each of its various components (general education, professional education, clinical education) and the lack of coordination between components and stages (preservice, induction, inservice). Lanier has carefully documented the diffuse nature of program responsibility and authority within colleges and universities, where everybody controls a piece of the action and where no single group is powerful enough to exert the kind of responsible leadership that might alter the status quo.[56] Clark and Marker describe the institutional arrangements within colleges and universities, as well as between these institutions and other stakeholders in teacher education, as providing a basic framework for "organizational irresponsibility."[57]

The curricula of both preservice and inservice teacher education programs often reflect the conflicts in function, authority, and responsibility within teacher education institutions and school systems, as well as the disharmony between institutions.[58] Lanier accurately summarizes the current status of the curricula in both preservice and inservice teacher education:

> The research is unequivocal about the general overall coursework provided for teachers. It remains casual at best and affords a poorly conceived collage of courses across the spectrum of initial preparation and an assembly of disparate content fragments throughout continuing education. The formal offerings lack curricular articulation within and between initial and continuing teacher education.[59]

At the preservice level, examples abound both in the RITE data and in the literature generally of the fragmented, compartmentalized nature of curricular offerings and the lack of coherent program foci. The ways authority and responsibility are assigned within teacher education programs often undermine efforts to integrate methods courses with clinical experiences and lead to fragmentation within clinical programs.[60]

At the inservice level, responsibility for staff development is widely scattered, with little attempt at coordination even when the various activities planned demand the time and energy of the same teachers.[61] Joyce has described professional development as a maze whose paths need to be charted with care:

> People working in professional development functions are isolated from one another organizationally and programmatically. Although there are many organizational elements which deal with professional development at the district, county, and state levels, there is little coordination.[62]

There is little question that the purposeful and articulated, ongoing, and developmental features of the RITE framework are in conflict with the current form of both preservice and inservice teacher education. Despite the fact that nonexemplars far outnumber programs that reflect the characteristics of the RITE reform, clinical teacher education practices do indeed exist that are consistent with the various critical features of the RITE framework. Many of the practices illustrated in the chapters by Borko, Copeland, and Ward give us hope that steps can be taken to see that these isolated examples come to represent modal practice in the field.

Little Investment in Research, Development, and Evaluation

The final distinguishing characteristic of teacher education today is the typically low investment in systematic research, development, and evaluation. Howey, for example, has concluded on the basis of a comprehensive national survey of preservice teacher preparation programs that research into and development of teacher education practice is rare in most of the institutions that prepare teachers.[63] Clark and Guba's study of knowledge production in schools and colleges of education, and Joyce and Clift's more general observations, support Howey's conclusion.[64] Relatively few schools and colleges of education are involved in a significant way in research related to any aspect of schooling, and a very minute portion of this scholarship has focused on the process of teacher education. At the inservice level, there appears to be consensus that there has been too little conceptually sound and methodologically rigorous research related to staff development, and too much reliance on personal experience and anecdotal reports.[65]

Cyphert and Spaights concluded after an extensive review of the literature that research and evaluation have had only a minimal impact on teacher education curricula, and that teacher education content and methods have been generated almost exclusively on logical grounds, with little reference to research and evaluation. Their statement about the content of teacher education programs remains as true today as it was twenty years ago:

> When one pursues the changes made in teacher education over the past 10 years, or projects ahead for the next decade, he is struck with the undeniable evidence that virtually all of those who are planning the "improvement" of teacher education are operating, and are likely to continue to operate, by applying their own subjective insight, hunches, and hypotheses growing out of experience to reorganize portions of their programs. . . . Too long many teacher educators have enjoyed the comfort of opinion without the discomfort of evidence.[66]

As Joyce and Clift point out, any innovation in teacher education, no matter how carefully thought out, requires knowledge production to test its strong and weak points and to make adjustments and improvements.[67] There are now no such efforts on a wide scale at either the preservice or inservice levels. The current scarcity of knowledge production within teacher education would inhibit the realization of the knowledge-based clinical programs called for by the RITE reform.

When one examines all four of these distinguishing characteristics of the context of teacher education (low status, limited investment of financial and human resources, fragmented and uncoordinated curriculum, and little investment in research and development) in relation to the critical features of the RITE framework, one cannot help being pessimistic about the potential for successful implementation of RITE clinical teacher education. For example, for a program of clinical teacher education to have an articulated purpose and to be ongoing and developmental (critical features of the RITE framework) would require substantial changes in the organizational structures in which roles are defined and status is awarded, given the fragmented, compartmentalized, and largely uncoordinated character of teacher education. The "strand of intention and activity that, over time and with concerted effort, provides a set of cumulative experiences aimed toward an articulated purpose" called for by Griffin in Chapter 1 (p. 17) seems hard to imagine given that the few whose roles would allow them to make this effort are those with the least political power within their organizations, and those least likely to be able to effect the kinds of fundamental changes needed.

Second, the lack of capability for knowledge production within the teacher education community bodes trouble for efforts to realize the knowledge-based features of the RITE framework, despite recent developments in codifying empirical and craft knowledge related to teaching. A knowledge-based clinical program must be able to operate on the basis of knowledge related to the clinical education of teachers, in addition to the various kinds of knowledge related to teaching discussed by Griffin. Here the evidence is overwhelming that the knowledge base related to clinical teacher education (its purposes, quality, and effects) is sorely lacking.[68] Although the RITE reform is based in part on The University of Texas Research and Development Center studies and on insights gained from the research literature in general, and although it offers some general guidance for clinical teacher educators, it does not provide the kinds of content- and context-specific knowledge that are needed to guide ongoing program development efforts.[69] This content- and context-specific knowledge can come only from ongoing efforts to monitor and evaluate the implementation of these innovations in specific contexts.

Three other aspects of the RITE framework merit mention in relation to the current contexts of clinical teacher education. First, the demand that clinical teacher education be context-related (the defining property of the RITE framework) calls for work environments that are conducive to teacher learning and growth. Among other things, these environments would be participatory and collaborative (e.g., characterized by professional collegiality) and would provide opportunities for reflection and analysis (two more of the critical features of the RITE framework).

There is little doubt of the absence of these characteristics in the lives of most preservice students, beginning teachers, and career teachers. For example, despite all of the rhetoric about the need for more participatory and collaborative forms of staff development, the involvement of teachers in the planning and design of staff development has been found to be largely symbolic, infrequent, and inconsequential.[70] Little argues that the conditions that are powerful enough to sustain collegial and participatory forms of staff development require a degree of organization, energy, skill, and endurance not now present in most school systems, and that the fit between organizational realities and key features of staff development such as collegiality is seductive yet essentially unrealizable under current conditions.[71] One hardly need mention the isolation of teachers and the lack of opportunities at both preservice and inservice levels for sustained reflection and analysis. The literature on the work lives of teachers paints a very clear picture of how current arrangements would make the participatory and collaborative and the analytic and reflective features of the RITE approach exceedingly difficult to accomplish.[72]

All of the evidence concerning the compatibility of the current contexts of clinical teacher education with the essential elements of the RITE framework suggests that the approach is likely to be implemented in a manner that would sustain the very practices it seeks to change—in a manner that would undermine the ethical roots of this approach in a commitment to teachers as professional decision-makers.

ETHICAL DIMENSIONS OF REFORM:
CLINICAL TEACHER EDUCATION AND
CONCEPTIONS OF THE TEACHER'S ROLE

As Crittenden correctly points out, the question of how teachers should be educated cannot be answered apart from taking a stand, implicitly or explicitly, on how much of the existing institutional form and social context of schooling should be accepted as given.[73] Either a program primarily integrates teachers into the logic of the present system and institutional arrangements, or it promotes a situation where teachers can deal critically with that reality in order to improve it. All curricular and programmatic decisions in teacher education need to be considered and ultimately justified on the basis of one of these directions.[74] As a significant part of this ethical dimension of teacher education, teacher educators decide priorities and make choices regarding the nature of the *teacher role* toward which teacher preparation is directed.[75]

One way to distinguish between the alternative conceptions of the teacher's role that necessarily undergird teacher education programs is to differentiate programs that seek to prepare teachers as *skilled craftspersons* from those that seek to prepare teachers as *professional decision-makers*.[76] An emphasis on preparing teachers who are (at best) skilled craftspersons places a priority on the development of proficiency in instruction and classroom management and, as Lanier points out, focuses attention on the behavioral performance of smoothly orchestrated routines and actions *within classrooms*.[77] Although there are many important differences among advocates of this view of teaching regarding the source and substance of the knowledge base that is to guide teachers,[78] none of them expresses any intent to prepare teachers who will be capable of assuming leadership in schools and school systems by becoming active participants in policy decisions that transcend individual classrooms. The teacher is viewed first and foremost as a skilled performer within the classroom, but is left dependent upon others for leadership and direction in determining the ends that are to be pursued in the classroom and school.

On the other hand, an emphasis on preparing teachers as professional decision-makers accepts the need to prepare teachers who are competent in the skills of instruction and classroom management, but seeks to supplement skilled craftsmanship with skill in the exercise of educational leadership. Here there is concern for teachers to play active roles in the shaping of educational environments, and for them to retain some control over the conception as well as the execution of their activities. Teacher education programs conducted on the basis of this view would emphasize the teacher's ability to exercise informed judgment about both the ends and the means of schooling, and would seek to prepare teachers who are willing and able to continue to learn about teaching throughout their careers.

All proposals for the education of teachers reflect some resolution of this issue regarding the degree of "occupational self-direction" that would be exerted by teachers, and the degree to which the workplace of the school should be an educative environment for teachers as well as for pupils. As discussed earlier, the RITE reform takes a very clear stand on this issue, and its framers are committed wholeheartedly to the education of teachers who are integrally involved in schoolwide decision-making, in making a contribution to the profession, and in the conceptualization as well as the execution of the work of teaching. Although Griffin's description of the ideal teacher in the opening chapter places the teacher-student relationship and pupil learning at the center of the teacher's role, and although the ideal teacher displays many elements of skilled craftsmanship, the RITE framework clearly goes beyond a commitment to skilled performance within the classroom and places a priority on the development of teachers as professional decision-makers and on the development of schools that sanction this conception of the teacher's role. On the other hand, the dominant view of the teacher in practice today throughout the United States is one of the teacher as (at best) a skilled craftsperson.[79]

The implementation of the RITE framework of clinical teacher education in particular situations will necessarily entail an emphasis on one or the other of these two conceptions of the teacher's role. Given the current institutional realities of teacher education described earlier (low status, little investment in resources, fragmented curriculum, and little investment in research, development, or evaluation) and the dominant view of the teacher as a skilled craftsperson, it is likely that implementation of the RITE framework will legitimate and sustain a conception of the teacher's role that is inconsistent with the RITE approach. Clinical teacher education programs do not now have the resources, personnel, or political power necessary for overcoming the dominance of nonexemplars of the RITE framework.

Two examples will illustrate how implementation of the RITE reform, even when the critical features of the model have technically been fulfilled, can lead to this ironic result. First, the *reflective and analytic* feature of the RITE framework requires that time be systematically set aside for teachers (together and alone) to reflect on their work in schools and classrooms and on their experiences in clinical teacher education programs. This emphasis on reflection and analysis stands in sharp contrast to current practice, where few such opportunities are provided to teachers. However, even to emphasize the importance of reflection and analysis does not address issues such as which aspects of practice are to form the basis of the analysis, at which level the analysis is to take place (e.g., the kinds of criteria to be employed), or the ends to which the analysis is to be directed. Reflection about teaching and schooling can take many forms and can work toward the preparation of teachers either as skilled craftspersons or as professional decision-makers, depending upon the form and substance of the reflection that occurs. For example, Van Mannen has identified three levels of reflection, each of which embraces different criteria for choosing among alternative courses of action. At the first level, *technical rationality*, the dominant concern is with the efficient and effective application of educational knowledge to attaining ends that are accepted as given. At this level, neither the ends nor the institutional contexts of the classroom and school are treated as problematic.

A second level of reflection, according to Van Mannen, is based upon a conception of *practical action*, where the problem is one of explicating and clarifying the assumptions and predispositions underlying an action and of assessing the educational consequences of that action. At this level, every action is seen as linked to particular value commitments, and the actor considers the worth of competing educational goals or ends.

The third and final level, *critical reflection*, incorporates consideration of moral and ethical criteria into the discourse about practical action. At this level, the central question becomes which educational goals, experiences, and activities lead toward just and equitable forms of life. Here both the teaching (ends and means) and the contexts in which teaching takes place are viewed as problematic.[80]

A commitment to the preparation of teachers as professional decision-makers, although focusing in part on reflection at the level of technical rationality, must also necessarily involve reflection and analysis at at least one of the other levels. Here, there is overwhelming evidence that when reflection and analysis have been provided for in the clinical education of teachers, there has been an almost exclusive focus on technical rationality even when lip service has been given to the importance of such things as critical thinking and teacher decision-making.[81] These opportunities for reflection and analysis, although technically fulfilling one of the critical features of the RITE framework, further the role of teachers as (at best) skilled craftspersons and deny teachers access to forms of rationality that would further the ethical commitments of the RITE reform. Implementation of the reflective and analytic feature of the RITE framework such that teachers are empowered to consider and to influence the ends and means of their work seems highly unlikely given the dominance of technical rationality and the role of teachers our society has been willing to support. We need to be clear that not every interpretation of "reflective and analytic" is consistent with the commitment of the RITE reform to the preparation of teachers as professional decision-makers.

A second feature of the RITE framework, that the clinical education of teachers be *knowledge-based*, acknowledges the importance of several different forms of knowledge (theoretical, propositional, empirical, and craft) and emphasizes the central role of craft knowledge in the clinical education of teachers. This feature requires that there be a reliance on some form of codified, verified, and reliable knowledge base in the formulation of clinical teacher education programs, as opposed to an exclusive reliance on idiosyncratic personal experience and anecdotal evidence. Here, as in the case of the reflective and analytic feature, the way in which the feature is interpreted is critical in determining the ethical consequences of implementation. Specifically, a clinical teacher education program can be knowledge-based according to the RITE criteria and further the development of teachers either as skilled craftspersons or as professional decision-makers, depending upon how the knowledge base is utilized.

Fenstermacher has described three ways teaching practice can be informed by educational knowledge: (1) by rules, (2) by evidence, and (3) by schemata. First, when the results of research, theories, and so on are converted into imperatives for teachers, educational knowledge is being used to inform teaching practice through rules. This highly prescriptive use of educational knowledge, with the passive role it assigns to teachers, is clearly contrary to the development of teachers as professional decision-makers and, as Fenstermacher argues, denies teachers a portion of their freedom to think and act independently.[82] Examples abound of the use of educational knowledge—of whatever type—in this manner.[83] It is important to note that acknowledging the central role of craft knowledge in the clinical education of teachers does not remove the danger of the prescriptive use of that knowledge. Unless clinical teacher education programs recognize and utilize the experience, insights, and expertise (i.e., craft knowledge) of teachers who are participating in a given program, these teachers will be relegated to passive roles in the educational process and will be denied access to the kinds of deliberations that would enhance their roles as professional decision-makers, regardless of reliance on the craft knowledge of other practitioners. The prescriptive use of craft knowledge in clinical teacher education programs is just as harmful to the teachers involved as the prescriptive use of other forms of knowledge.

Using educational knowledge as evidence or schemata to inform teaching practice is more consistent with the role of the teacher as a professional decision-maker. Educational knowledge is used as evidence when, for example, the results of empirical research are used to help teachers test the beliefs they hold about their work or, as Fenstermacher argues, to encourage the transformation of teachers' beliefs from subjectively to objectively reasonable. Using knowledge as evidence does not require that teachers modify their beliefs every time they come into contact with educational knowledge. It only requires that teachers (who are accorded the status of thinking, reasoning persons) weigh seriously the implications of that knowledge for their own work. Finally, the use of educational knowledge as schemata provides teachers with new concepts and new ways to grasp in descriptive and explanatory ways the features of their work.[84]

Although several teacher educators have recently argued forcefully against the prescriptive use of educational knowledge as rules (e.g., in research-based teacher training), and although examples exist of the use of educational knowledge in ways that do support teachers as professional decision-makers, the prescriptive approach still dominates teacher education at both the preservice and inservice levels. Here, again, we need to be clear that not all interpretations of the knowledge-based feature of the RITE framework of clinical teacher education are consistent with its ethical commitments.

Other examples could easily be provided of how the particular meaning given to a critical feature of the RITE framework is significant in determining the ethical consequences of implementation. Each critical feature of the RITE framework can be interpreted and implemented in a variety of ways, only some of which are consistent with the development of teachers as professional decision-makers. And, in each case, the most likely interpretations to be implemented are those that are inconsistent with the commitments of the RITE approach. If RITE clinical teacher education is to further the preparation of teachers as professional decision-makers, then careful steps need to be taken to ensure that its implementation works toward the realization of interpretations of the critical feature of the RITE framework that are consistent with its ethical commitments.

RECOMMENDATIONS FOR IMPLEMENTING CLINICAL TEACHER EDUCATION

Because of the discrepancies between the dominant traditions and values in teacher education and the ethical commitments of the RITE reform, it is important for teacher educators to plan the implementation of RITE clinical teacher education carefully to account for the institutional realities of teacher education. Fullan and Pomfret suggest four factors which influence the course of the implementation of educational innovations: (1) the characteristics of the innovation (e.g., its explicitness and complexity); (2) the characteristics of the institutions in which the innovation is to be implemented; (3) the strategies used to introduce and implement the innovation (e.g., staff development resources); and (4) the characteristics of macro-sociopolitical factors outside of the institutions in which the innovation is to be implemented.[85] These "determinants" of implementation suggest three general guidelines for the implementation of the RITE framework of clinical teacher education.

First, the implementation of RITE clinical teacher education needs to involve fundamental changes in the values and traditions of teacher education, if we want to avoid a situation where the RITE reform is assimilated into institutional patterns of behavior and belief. Romberg and Price's distinction between ameliorative and radical innovation is useful in clarifying the kinds of changes needed. An *ameliorative innovation* is designed to make some ongoing practice better or more efficient, but does not challenge the cultural traditions of the institutions in which the innovation is to be implemented. On the other hand, a *radical innovation* challenges and confronts conventional patterns of belief and practice and the cultural traditions that underlie them.[86] The analysis presented in this chapter has suggested the need for the RITE reform to be a radical innovation, one that leads to a fundamental reconceptualization of the clinical education of teachers. This necessity for cultural change in the implementation of RITE clinical teacher education leads to the first recommendation for implementation: *Teacher educators should identify and anticipate the traditions in belief, practice, and organizational arrangements that need to be challenged in the implementation of RITE clinical teacher education and plan for these changes.*

Fullan and Pomfret argue that the more complex and ambiguous an innovation, the more difficult it is to accomplish implementation successfully.[87] The RITE reform is clearly rather ambiguous in that it allows for multiple interpretations of its critical attributes, and rather complex in that it requires the simultaneous implementation of all seven of its critical features. When these characteristics are viewed in the context of a politically weak and fragmented teacher education community whose dominant values and norms are in conflict with the ethical basis of the reform, the task of successful implementation seems overwhelming indeed.

However difficult this task may seem, it is still manageable under certain conditions. The first and most important condition for effecting change in teacher education is for teacher educators to recognize and criticize the cultural traditions that need to be challenged. This is not to romanticize the power of this essentially analytic activity to transform concrete reality. But we will never begin to break the cycle of patchwork and surface-level reforms that have characterized teacher education throughout its history until we identify and challenge the unexamined traditions that have subverted reforms in the past. In the present instance this includes being as clear about what is *not* an example of RITE clinical teacher education as about what *is* consistent with the ethical commitments of the reform.

The second recommendation for implementation follows from Fullan and Pomfret's caution to pay careful attention to the ways in which an innovation is introduced and implemented: *Teacher educators should try to ensure that the implementation process models the critical features of the reform itself.* It is extremely important that all participants understand the values and assumptions underlying the innovation and its various components, and that they be committed to implementing the ethical principles of the reform. An implementation strategy which is itself purposeful and articulated, participatory and collaborative, context-responsive, and developmental will facilitate dissolving the fragmentation, lack of coordination, and low commitment that characterize the clinical education of teachers today. Such a strategy will maximize the chances for the essence of the reform to be implemented and for the commitment of personnel to be engaged. RITE clinical teacher education cannot be successfully implemented by administrative fiat or by other means that violate the principles of the reform itself. The critical attributes of the RITE framework for the clinical education of teachers are also critical ingredients in the process of its implementation. If the implementation process is also to model the critical features of a reflective and analytic and a knowledge-based program, then teacher educators will need to ensure that a systematic monitoring procedure is planned and carried out to evaluate the effects (anticipated or not) of the implementation process so that a context-specific knowledge base of clinical teacher education underlies the process of reform. Unless teacher educators can exemplify all of the critical attributes in the process of implementation, they will be undermining the RITE framework by their example. All of this will require substantial changes in role relationships, organizational structures, and patterns of resource allocation, as illustrated in the ensuing chapter by Ward and Griffin.

The final recommendation for the implementation of the RITE framework of clinical teacher education follows from the politically weak position of teacher education within the institutions in which it is carried out and in relation to the external agencies and organizations that exert influence on the process: *Teacher educators should assume a more aggressive political stance in relation to the organizations and agencies that allocate resources and rewards affecting teacher education programs and the professional careers of teacher educators.* Throughout the history of teacher education, teacher educators have adopted an essentially reactive and apolitical position in relation to those groups that set the parameters for the content of teacher education programs, and they have accepted the low status that has been accorded them. There have been numerous analyses of how both internal university and school system policies and external policies related to certification and accreditation have served as impediments to reform in teacher education.[88] If the changes required by the RITE reform are to be realized, greater priority in the form of resources and incentives will need to be given to the clinical education of teachers and to those teacher educators who conduct it. The *only* avenue open to obtain these resources is through the political arena.

This chapter has attempted to present a realistic evaluation of the difficulties that lie ahead in the implementation of the RITE framework of clinical teacher education. Although concrete examples of each of the various attributes of the RITE framework already exist, and although the framework will probably have high appeal for the majority of teacher educators, the institutional realities of teacher education could, if not fundamentally altered, lead to the assimilation of the framework into current patterns of belief and practice. On the other hand, despite all of the obstructions that lie ahead, we have every reason to be optimistic for the future of RITE clinical teacher education. The time is right for the kind of fundamental reform in teacher education called for by the RITE framework. Never before in our history has attention been focused on the education of teachers as it has today. Never before has the climate been so ripe for fundamental cultural change in teacher education. We should be careful not to lose this opportunity for reform by repeating the mistakes of our past. One way to avoid repeating the unproductive history of reform in teacher education is to attend to the social and ethical dimensions of the reform process.

6

The Policy and Decision-Making Contexts of Reform in Clinical Teacher Education

Beatrice A. Ward • Gary A. Griffin

This book has presented a research-based conception of clinical teacher education. The conception is seen as a means to radically and positively alter the preparation, induction, and professional development of teachers. Examples of how this change might appear in practice illustrate both the prospects and the dilemmas of moving toward implementation of the RITE framework.

A common problem associated with proposals for dramatic reform in any large-scale enterprise such as teacher education is that such proposals are often unaccompanied by acknowledgement of the policy and decision-making activities that must accompany any attempt at implementation. Although we do not claim that this chapter is a comprehensive treatment of the myriad issues that must be confronted, we do believe it is important to our intentions to set forth a number of items for consideration. The remainder of this chapter attempts to clarify issues related to policy and decision-making such as (1) the place of clinical teacher education in a more comprehensive view of professional education, (2) the particular knowledge most central to the RITE framework, (3) implementation considerations for colleges and universities, school systems, and state and regional bodies, (4) how the framework will impact certification of teachers, (5) the relation of the framework to considerations of teaching as a profession, (6) how the framework can influence teacher evaluation systems, (7) the need for multiple-organization collaboration prior to and during implementation, and (8) specific support requirements for successful implementation and adoption.

PROFESSIONAL EDUCATION AND CLINICAL TEACHER EDUCATION

In this book we have attempted to describe and justify a vitally important component of professional education, clinical teacher education. As implied throughout the volume, clinical education is the aspect of professional education that distinguishes it from more conventional education programs. The opportunities to learn from and about the "doing" of professional activity occur in classrooms and schools for teachers, clinics and hospitals for doctors, and social service agencies for social workers, to mention only a few. The importance of clinical education is claimed for all professions.

However, clinical teacher education is but one part of a comprehensive program to prepare teachers and provide growth opportunities for new and career teachers. Other major categories of teacher education include academic studies, professional studies, professional organization studies, and independent studies.

Academic studies are those programs of instruction that teachers engage in for the purpose of learning about and maintaining knowledge and skill related to their academic disciplines. Teachers of mathematics, for example, take courses in mathematics at colleges and universities to become expert in their fields and to keep up with advances in theoretical and practical aspects of mathematics. The same is true for teachers of the arts, sciences, and humanities. Clinical teacher education provides opportunities for teacher candidates and teachers to demonstrate that they know their subject areas but—importantly—also requires that they know how to transform that knowledge so that students gain access to it.

Academic studies are typically either preparatory or advanced. Preparatory studies usually occur in undergraduate programs, whereas advanced studies usually lead to master's or doctoral degrees. Although it has been conventional practice for a student to graduate with a baccalaureate degree accompanied by recommendation for a teaching certificate, as in the case of the secondary teacher education candidate who majors in French and takes a concentration of education courses to qualify for graduation and teaching certification, there is a growing belief that teachers should major in a discipline, receive a bachelor's degree, and *then* take courses that lead toward teacher certification. Certain of these proposals suggest that the teaching concentration should lead to a second degree, a Master of Arts, for example, whereas others would add a "fifth year" of study leading to the usual bachelor's degree. The assumption underlying all of these proposals is that teachers must be expert in their knowledge of their subject matter and that such expertise is best accomplished through concentrated exposure to the nature of a discipline.

How to transform this knowledge of subject matter is the proper focus of *professional studies*. Although there are proponents of the belief that teaching rests solely upon knowledge of subject matter, we take the position that there is a growing body of knowledge about how to plan for and present subject matter, how to engage students with the content so that learning occurs and can be demonstrated, and how to assess the learner's grasp of the discipline under consideration. These studies include curriculum planning, pedagogical practice, diagnosis and prescription for students, test-making, remediation, and evaluation. Professional studies also attend to developing in the teacher a deep and wide understanding of learner characteristics, matches between teaching and learning styles, and the selection of age- and grade-appropriate materials of instruction.

Currently, attention has been drawn to including in the professional studies component of teacher education programs the research-derived conception of the school as a social organization. Study of this area is seen as an important adjunct to clinical teacher education because it provides the novice and the experienced teacher with a better understanding of the sources, manifestations, and consequences of what have come to be called "conditions of work." Furthermore, its inclusion provides a knowledge base for clinical activity.

Here is an illustration of how knowledge of school organization drawn from professional study "fits" with clinical teacher education. Two teachers participated in a short-term exercise aimed at understanding why they taught as they did. They were observed by an "expert," who shared the written narratives of the observations with them, accompanied by conversations about their teaching. In the course of the conversations, it became clear that the teachers were more than somewhat uncomfortable and dissatisfied with what they saw as encroachments on their professional autonomy. That is, they believed that the school and the district had made uncalled-for demands that they teach by using specific standardized lesson plans, by requiring student completion of commercially-developed worksheets, and by engaging in uniform testing procedures.

These two teachers only dimly perceived how such decisions were made — what intellectual and political tradeoffs were part of the decision-making process, the relationships between teachers and the administrators who either supported or questioned such standardization, and so forth. In the same school district, however, other teachers, far more sensitive to schools as social organizations, mounted a campaign to exempt their school from the district procedures. They enlisted school administration in their efforts, used the teacher organization as an ally to support their position, provided evidence to central office administrators of the effectiveness of different instructional practices, and eventually gained acceptance from the district officers for school-level decision-making about such teaching activities. Clearly, the teachers in this school had a sophisticated understanding of how the school as an organization works and of how to use that knowledge to realize their own professional purposes.

Professional studies can take place in school settings as well as in colleges and universities. The attention being given to staff development as a school-district responsibility, for instance, is an indication that continued professional growth is increasingly seen as an important function of the employers of teachers. A key challenge for the growing number of such district programs is to eliminate the one-shot workshop, the single speech by a visiting dignitary, and administrivia-laden approaches, and to replace them with comprehensive, needs-based, ongoing professional studies.

Professional organization studies are growing in number and gaining increased status within educational settings. These are opportunities to learn about teaching through courses, workshops, and other learning activities that are provided by the teacher unions and the associations within subject areas. In recent years, the American Federation of Teachers (AFT) and the National Education Association (NEA) have shown greater sensitivity than in the past to the professional growth needs of their members. National, regional, and local union meetings are often devoted to finding ways to expose members to new knowledge that has direct bearing upon their work as teachers. The AFT, for example, has developed a strategy for preparing selected members to deliver to other members the latest research on teaching findings. Similarly, the NEA is providing significant financial support to the initiation of school-based school improvement efforts. Likewise, teachers of English, foreign languages, social studies, and other subjects can tap into their professional associations for the purpose of upgrading their knowledge and skills in their subject areas.

Independent studies are those inquiries engaged in, alone or with others, by the teacher who wants to know more about and be more skillful in teaching. These studies are often particular to an idiosyncratic problem (e.g., how to deal with a specific student in one's class) or to an issue not currently addressed by a teacher's district, college, or professional organization (e.g., finding the best ways to develop team teaching for limited-English-speaking special education students). It is important to recognize that, whatever the source of the issue and however the issue is addressed, professional career teachers engage in independent study regularly in their teaching lives. In fact, if the clinical teacher education framework proposed in this book achieves its anticipated outcomes, this form of professional growth will become more prevalent as a correlate to teacher reflection and analysis, a feature and goal of the framework.

Clearly, then, clinical teacher education as presented here is part of a larger conception of professional education for teachers. It is necessary, we believe, but not sufficient to provide the intellectual and practical foundations for excellence in teaching. Clinical teacher education must be buttressed by academic studies, professional studies, participation in growth opportunities provided by professional organizations, and individual professional inquiry.

DECISIONS ABOUT THE KNOWLEDGE ON WHICH RITE CLINICAL TEACHER EDUCATION IS BASED

As emphasized in the previous chapters, the content and processes of RITE clinical teacher education are knowledge-based. Knowledge gained from research on effective teaching and effective teacher education provides a strong foundation for the RITE framework. The technical knowledge and expertise teachers develop as they work with students over time adds to the array of instructional insights, skills, and strategies made available to teachers. And knowledge about effective performance of non-classroom professional teacher roles contributes to the ongoing development of experienced teachers.

To illustrate, consider the teaching characteristic "clarity of instruction." In numerous research studies, teacher clarity has been found to be related to student performance. However, these studies have identified no one way to achieve clarity. The characteristics of the students being taught, the curricular and instructional boundaries within which the teacher works, the instructional materials available for use in the classroom, and the way a teacher organizes the classroom are among the contextual factors that may influence the steps, explanations, and other strategies that will make objectives, concepts, and learning procedures clear to students. Furthermore, research reports typically provide few, if any, examples of what the teachers who achieved clarity actually did. Thus, the technical expertise of experienced teachers is needed to provide exemplars. These teachers can describe and model the actions they take to achieve clarity, thereby providing a range of approaches to clarification of content and procedures that other teachers may employ. They can also coach other teachers in implementing various strategies. Because the strategies probably will have been developed in the same schools in which the teachers who are participating in the training teach, they are likely to be workable in that particular context.

It would be difficult to argue with the strength of teacher development based upon knowledge about effective teaching and effective teacher education, as compared with training based on faddism or trial-and-error learning.

The use of multiple knowledge bases heightens the relevance and usefulness of the skills, knowledge, and insights that teachers acquire. Yet, over time, a program that is presently based upon the best that is known about effective teaching and teacher development can become out-of-date, can fail to respond to changes in context, can become too dependent upon one knowledge base versus another, and can allow fads and untested opinions regarding teaching to reduce the soundness of the training that occurs.

To assure that teacher development continues to build from solid and useful information, policymakers and practitioners need to give their attention to several factors. The first is maintenance of the knowledge base so that teachers work with the most current and most relevant knowledge. Another is the provision of mechanisms whereby the technical knowledge that is obtained and used in clinical teacher education programs becomes part of the general knowledge base for effective teaching and is disseminated to all professional educators and policymakers. A third is design of a procedure for making decisions about what knowledge should drive a particular teacher education program, given the developmental accomplishments of the teachers who will participate and the context(s) in which new skills and knowledge will be applied.

Maintenance of the knowledge base.   During the past decade, research on teaching and teacher education has received strong support from the U. S. Department of Education, particularly the department's National Institute of Education. The knowledge upon which RITE and other clinical teacher education programs now can build was created largely as a result of this support. Presently, there is concern that this high level of interest in and support for research-based knowledge about effective teaching is diminishing. Even though research and development centers for teaching and teaching policy were among the centers included recently in a national competition, funding for individual research outside these centers appears to be decreasing.

Hence, maintenance of an updated knowledge base about effective teaching and teacher education is a two-pronged issue. On one hand, allocation of national (and perhaps state) funds to support new research is essential. In this chapter alone, we have pointed out several areas in which additional research is needed to guide use of the RITE framework. On the other hand, new information must continue to be made available to the individual engaged in clinical teacher education. Accomplishment of both of these ends requires legislative action followed by the design of an agenda for use of the support that is provided. This agenda may include new research questions and new dissemination activities. It may continue current areas of inquiry and national dissemination efforts that are already in place. The key requirements at the national and state level are (1) ongoing support for production of more and better knowledge about teaching and teacher development, and (2) regular support for dissemination activities, such as the clearinghouse for research on teacher education as well as conferences and publications, all of which bring practitioners together with new research knowledge about effective teaching and teacher education.

Gaining access to technical knowledge. As teachers participate in clinical training to increase their teaching skills and knowledge, they use many of the insights and techniques they have developed, applied, and refined over time in their classrooms (technical knowledge) to aid them in interpreting and applying the new research-based knowledge. The illustration presented earlier of training in clarity of instruction suggested ways for making the technical knowledge of one teacher in a program available to others in that program. The challenge is to dispense this same knowledge to other clinical programs that are focusing upon similar aspects of teaching and teacher development.

Furthermore, the analytic and reflective feature of the RITE framework requires teachers to conduct their own inquiries into effective teaching as small-scale, single-classroom research studies. But as long as the insights and understandings about effective instruction gained through analysis of what happens in the classroom and reflection upon student performance remain only with the individual teacher, the general knowledge base on teaching fails to benefit.

Gaining access to the technical knowledge of teachers throughout the nation calls for creative action. For example, within a single clinical teacher education program, teachers could be asked to share the recent insights, understandings, and modifications of instruction they consider most important to the improvement of their teaching. Someone from the program staff (a teacher or teacher educator) could compile this information and look for common insights and understandings, creative modifications of instruction that solved problems of concern to several teachers, as well as unresolved problems that might be likely topics for future clinical teacher development.

These same activities could be raised to the level of a regional collaborative effort to which teachers from several training programs would contribute information. Participants in clinical programs serving teachers who work in similar instructional contexts could be brought together from across the nation to share and compile technical knowledge.

However, the real issue surrounding technical knowledge about effective teaching is one of value and priority rather than access and dissemination. To date, the vast majority of researchers in education still consider such knowledge to be "soft" and "situation-specific." Perhaps compilation and reporting of cross-teacher findings will help alleviate some of this doubt. Use of teachers' technical knowledge in successful school improvement projects may persuade some researchers of the importance of this knowledge base. But, in the long run, the educators for whom technical knowledge will be most important are likely to be those engaged in collaborative design and conduct of teaching and of clinical teacher education. Therefore, information acquisition and dissemination should be focused on these educators and the professional organizations and other agencies that are most apt to reach them.

Decisions about knowledge to be used in a clinical teacher education program. Whether based on new research knowledge or on technical knowledge compiled across teachers, in order to avoid the pitfalls mentioned earlier, each clinical teacher education program should establish a process whereby the knowledge upon which the program builds is revisited every three to five years.

If new research findings are available, the review should include periodic perusal of this new information. If not, technical knowledge may be the primary source for updating the goals, content, and processes of the program. Regardless, the review should include examination of both the old and the new knowledge bases. The relevance and appropriateness of the knowledge should be reassessed based on the demands, circumstances, and conditions currently prevailing in the local educational context. The developmental needs of the teachers in the program also should be reviewed, and the knowledge base adopted to these needs.

Teachers, researchers, teacher educators, and representatives of professional organizations within a given locale should collaboratively generate a new knowledge base. This base may include some, all, or none of the old and the new knowledge, depending upon the current instructional context and the developmental requirements of the teachers.

To assure such revisiting of the knowledge base, a clinical teacher education program should include specific program renewal timelines and procedures. The mechanisms for leadership and inter-agency collaborations discussed in other sections of this chapter offer means for accomplishing these efforts. Policy requirements for continued support of a program can mandate such renewal. And the process will be aided by multiple perspectives, a variety of skills and expertise, and open minds.

IMPLEMENTATION OF
RITE CLINICAL TEACHER EDUCATION

In preceding chapters, the authors have indicated that large-scale implementation of the RITE clinical teacher education framework as an integral part of university or school-district teacher development programs will be a challenge. Zeichner goes so far as to propose that implementation will be difficult even in places where current teacher training programs incorporate several of the framework's features. Nonetheless, the authors also argue for the importance of the framework. They provide examples of the ways teacher education would be conducted based on the framework. They suggest how current preservice, induction, and professional teacher education programs could be modified and expanded to increase their responsiveness to the RITE requirements.

Therefore, it is reasonable to conclude that use of the RITE framework to improve teachers' growth, development, and performance beginning with the day they enter a preservice program and extending for the duration of their professional careers is both desirable and possible. Still, based on what is known about the institutions in which the education will occur and about the requirements for successful implementation of complex educational improvements, it also is evident that wide-scale use of the RITE framework cannot be left to chance.

Two implementation requirements, in particular, underline the need for a planned approach to the introduction of RITE clinical teacher education. One is the application of the framework to all phases of a teacher's career and the requirement that teacher education be planned and conducted in an ongoing, developmental manner spanning this career. Enthusiastic selling of the framework by a single individual in a single institution (school, school district, or university) may introduce it into one specific teacher development effort, but will fall short of providing RITE clinical education at all stages of teacher development and will fail to achieve the ongoing, developmental, planned approach to teacher development that underlies the framework.

The second requirement is centered in the importance the RITE framework gives to individual teacher development and growth. Currently, teacher education programs and the standards applied in certification and evaluation of teacher performance emphasize achievement of the same, or similar, knowledge and skills by all teachers. Tension between these existing goals and expectations and the RITE clinical teacher education commitment to furthering the growth of individual teachers who already have mastered these basic skills may complicate, if not hinder, implementation of the RITE framework.

To accomplish broad-scale use of RITE clinical teacher education thus requires that practitioners and policymakers (a) attend to where and how leadership is provided for implementation of the framework and anticipate conflicts with institutional structures, and (b) create procedures that accommodate individual teacher development and at the same time assure that all teachers possess the basic skills of teaching.

Leadership for implementation across multiple agencies. As suggested above, at a maximum level of productivity, RITE clinical teacher education brings together in a single teacher development effort the full range of activities and responsibilities, some of which are currently assigned to universities and colleges, some to school districts, some to teacher organizations, and some to intermediate/regional service agencies.

Unfortunately, few in the teacher education arena (e.g., university-based teacher educators or school-district-based staff developers) have had experience with such cross-institutional efforts, let alone with implementation of a program such as this. Previous improvements in teacher education have concentrated largely on one stage of teacher development and have involved major change in only one institution. For example, when competency-based preservice teacher education programs were introduced, university programs changed, but school districts made few changes in the staff development that was provided once a teacher was employed. Similarly, school-based teacher development tied to school improvement has altered the way school districts conduct inservice teacher education but has lead to few, if any, changes in university and college preservice teacher education programs.

Hence, to achieve the desired reform in the clinical aspects of teacher education calls for leadership that crosses institutional boundaries. This, in turn, raises such questions as: Who provides the impetus for improvement? Who requires that the necessary changes be made in the programs of each institution? Who provides encouragement and reward for achieving the desired improvements within each institution? Is one person given responsibility for the improvement effort? Where is such leadership located?

Among the variety of possible ways university chancellors or presidents, school-district superintendents, and professional organization leaders can support introduction of RITE clinical teacher education, the most promising step to take appears to be the creation of a new professional role. This role can be conceptualized as that of a single individual responsible for ensuring that the RITE features are met in the clinical teacher education provided by all collaborating universities, colleges, and school districts, and funded jointly by all these institutions. Alternatively, we can envision the role of such an individual in each institution. Under the latter arrangement, the person responsible for introduction and maintenance of the RITE framework as a legitimate and functional part of teacher education in a school district, for example, would work with those with similar responsibilities in the universities and colleges in which the majority of new teachers selected by the school district were trained, with a similar person in the professional teachers' organization that represented the teachers in the district, with a similar person in any regional agency that conducted teacher education activities for the school district, and with such a person in the state educational agency responsible for certification and recertification of teachers. All of these people would work together to plan, develop, and provide teacher education that met the requirements of the RITE framework, provided growth and development for the entire professional lives of the teachers, was coordinated across all the institutions, and assured that teachers who participated were certified to perform professional teaching duties in the district's schools.

In addition, a person in one of these roles could facilitate implementation of the RITE framework by maintaining a focus on the need for improvement of the teacher development efforts conducted at all stages of a teacher's career; by encouraging and supporting professors, teachers, and others who participate in the introduction of the framework; by assuring that teachers collaborate and participate in the design and conduct of whatever program is carried out; and by calling the attention of relevant policymakers and administrators to improvements and changes in requirements for teacher credentials at various points in a teaching career.

To establish such a role and to further the implementation of the RITE framework calls for action by legislatures and policy boards. For example, a state board of education and a state board of regents might provide funds for special planning efforts or require submission of plans for bringing universities and school districts together to build teacher education programs that attend to the features of the RITE framework. Presently, legislative reforms, particularly at the state level, tend to include directives as to the skills and knowledge a teacher must possess in order to be employed in a school in the state, and as to how this capability will be evaluated. They are less precise regarding improvement of the preparation itself and designation of the institutions that should be involved. For RITE clinical teacher education to become part of the teacher development system will require action on "how to do it" as well as on "what to teach."

Sameness of teacher role definition versus individual teacher growth and development. The bulk of current teacher education programs and practices at the preservice, induction, and professional stages of teaching stress development of a common set of skills and knowledge by all participants. Furthermore, except within a few recent master/mentor teacher programs, most teachers assume the same responsibilities and perform the same functions throughout their professional careers. A first-year teacher and a teacher with thirty years' experience are expected to do the same things. Even when a more effective effort at any of the career stages has incorporated some RITE features such that it is, for example, knowledge-based, purposeful and articulated, and participatory and collaborative, differences in participants' knowledge and skills and in their experience bases seldom lead to differences in the activities that are provided. Furthermore, general teacher preparation gives little attention to the differences in the contexts in which teachers might teach.

The RITE framework underlines the importance of attending to both context and differences between teachers in the design and conduct of the clinical aspects of teacher education. Having posed these requirements, we hasten to point out that the framework does not call for elimination of all large- or small-group teacher preparation efforts. The framework does call for inclusion of individual as well as group growth opportunities. It promotes differentiation of teacher roles and responsibilities across a teaching career.

Reconceptualization of clinical teacher education as a multi-faceted process will help to alleviate the tension between our present view of teacher education and the one posed by the framework. It is appropriate for teacher education to include some experiences in which teachers at a particular career stage (or in a particular instance, across stages) are introduced to, practice, and implement the same set of new skills and knowledge. For example, all science teachers in a school district or region might be taught to use new laboratory procedures and equipment. All teachers in a school might receive assistance in the use of cooperative groups as a teaching/learning strategy. At the same time, a smaller number of teachers within a school, grade level, school district, or region might come together to build expertise in observation and coaching of teachers who are in the induction stage of their careers. Meanwhile, an individual teacher might participate in a university symposium on new knowledge regarding how students learn to read.

When the RITE framework is fully implemented, teacher education no longer will be a single set of activities provided throughout a school district by a staff development office. Teachers will participate and collaborate in the design of the programs in which they will engage. Any one, or a combination, of the institutions involved in clinical teacher education may provide the training. More experienced teachers often will serve as leaders. Individual teachers will work with the person in the new role described here to build growth and development plans and to identify opportunities that support their acquisition of needed skills and knowledge.

TEACHER CERTIFICATION

A major issue in the redefinition of clinical teacher education is the relation of the framework to initial certification and recertification of teachers by state education departments. Conventionally, teacher candidates are certified to teach after they have either completed a course of study that has been approved by an appropriate state agency and whose graduates are automatically certified, or presented for examination relevant academic and experiential evidence closely approximating that which would have been accrued as a consequence of participation in an approved program. The certification rests upon agreement that the teacher candidate has experienced what is believed to be "effective" teacher preparation. Recertification is that process used in some states whereby teachers are required to provide proof at varying points in their careers that they have continued to grow in their teaching roles. This recertification might occur once (after which the teacher is given a lifetime credential) or more than once, say every five or ten years of service.

The inherent conceptual and practical difficulties in this process are compounded when numbers of teachers are needed but sufficient numbers of certified teachers are unavailable, as occurred in the post-World War II years and as is anticipated for the early 1990s. In these times it becomes common practice for selected system officers to search for and appoint candidates to teach who have some other qualification, perhaps a baccalaureate degree in one of the subject matter disciplines, or perhaps experience in day care centers or other child-oriented agencies. Even though these people may have only what are called "emergency certificates," they become teachers.

Whether in the best of times when it is business as usual, or in difficult times such as when emergency certificates must be issued, certification is a central piece of the action in teacher education. If state boards of education are unclear in their specifications of what is good teacher education (in program approval), it is possible that questionable practices could characterize teacher education programs. If teachers are recertified as a consequence of only cursory examination, such as of whether or not they have earned a master's degree at an accredited institution, there may not be any relation between the degree and teaching excellence. If almost any college-educated person can be appointed to a classroom post — even if it is a time of personnel emergency — there is even less likelihood that the so-called teacher will meet the criteria for the ideal teacher described earlier.

Naturally, we believe that certification and recertification should depend upon evidence that the candidate has engaged in the kinds of clinical experiences that we have advanced in the RITE framework and elaborated in the separate chapters dealing with preservice, induction, and inservice teacher education. This is not a hollow belief, nor is it one that we put forward out of blind loyalty to the framework. It is a belief that emerged as a consequence of the growing body of evidence that supports the claims made in this book.

We believe all the more that certification needs to be supported by the RITE framework when we consider the socio-political environment within which certification issues are debated, decided, and implemented. That arena has not, in the past, been overly informed by solid research-based propositions. Instead, it has been seen as a sort of trading post wherein ideological positions are exchanged for authority to certify. Furthermore, given the number of teacher education institutions in the country — currently estimated at 1,300 — such tradeoffs tend to reduce expectations for teacher preparation and continued growth to a level of mediocrity, a lowest-common-denominator form of criterion building and application.

We are not so naive as to believe that installation of the features of the RITE framework as determinants of teacher education program approval will extinguish all of the ills of teacher education. But we do believe that careful attention to the framework, its specific elements, and its relationship to other teacher education program components will strengthen the intellectual basis for making the vital decisions related to providing qualified teachers for the nation's children and youth.

Sameness of certification requirements versus individual teacher growth and development. One aspect of implementation of the RITE framework that has particular implications for certification issues is its emphasis on individual teacher development. Currently, certification requirements give little attention to the fact that teachers teach in different contexts and that the skills and knowledge required for excellence in teaching may differ depending upon the context in which a teacher teaches. (Note: Certain special training programs and credentials, such as those for bilingual teacher certification, do consider context.) Once the RITE framework is institutionalized, teacher certification requirements may become multi-faceted. All teachers may be expected to demonstrate that they possess some basic teaching skills. Additional knowledge and skill requirements will be appropriate to the context in which a teacher is employed to teach and thus may differ from teacher to teacher. Furthermore, requirements for a teacher who will serve as both a mentor teacher and a classroom teacher may differ from those for someone who is a classroom teacher only.

Ultimately, in support of and response to wide-scale use of RITE clinical teacher education, policymakers may not stipulate a particular examination, a particular evaluation format, or completion of a particular set of courses as proof that a person is prepared to function effectively in a teaching situation. Rather, policies may require that a teacher submit a plan that includes (a) evidence of the teaching skills and knowledge the teacher has already acquired, (b) designation of the skills, knowledge, and experience the teacher is to acquire next in order to continue to grow and develop, (c) evidence that the program in which the teacher will engage includes the RITE framework features, and (d) evidence that the school district in which the teacher is employed and other agencies collaborating in conduct of clinical teacher education in that district are utilizing and extending the professional skills of the teacher.

Such an approach accommodates the importance for all teachers to possess certain basic teaching skills, and the equally important need to (a) recognize individual differences among teachers and teaching settings, and (b) build professional career opportunities for teachers.

TEACHING AS A PROFESSION

Despite some claims to the contrary, the rhetoric surrounding teaching has historically included reference to teachers as professionals. Although certain hallmarks of professional status continue to be absent from teaching (e.g., autonomy of practice, confidentiality between client and professional), evidence has emerged that teaching is moving toward increased professional status. One sign of this change is the development of a growing knowledge base for "best teaching practice" that is not conventionally available to those outside the teaching profession. Although there will probably always be debates about what is to be valued in teachers and teaching, there is mounting scientific evidence about the relationships between teaching behaviors and student outcomes, largely as a consequence of the research sponsored by the National Institute of Education during the 1970s and 1980s.

Another phenomenon associated with the rise of professionalism in teaching is the changing stance of teacher unions in relation to such issues as demonstration of teaching competence, peer review, programs of professional development, and educational reform initiatives, particularly career ladders. Perhaps of most importance to the professional status of teachers is the attention being given to peer review and career ladders.

Peer review assumes that teachers have the necessary knowledge to determine whether or not other teachers are using desired practices. Peer review is a step toward assuming greater control over entry into and continuation in the profession. The assumption of responsibility for the practices of fellow professionals is a central tenet of professionalism. Likewise, to consider career ladders for teachers is to break away from the untenable assumption that "a teacher is a teacher is a teacher" that undergirds certain defensive postures related to the growth of teaching expertise.

Although there are other examples of this move toward the professionalization of teaching, these two will serve as exemplars in advancing reasons to implement the clinical teacher education framework presented in this volume. Because the framework calls for a knowledge base to guide decision-making, it demands that participants in teacher development programs determine what knowledge and skills are of most value in teaching. This determination would be of great value to peer review proposals (and, in fact, to most evaluation schemes) because it would create a mirror against which teachers' competence could be measured. This is true for pedagogical knowledge and skill as well as for what is the focus of the first wave of teacher testing, basic skill knowledge.

The career ladder proposals need, for effective implementation, a differentiation of teaching roles and a specification of minimum and maximum performance of those roles. The framework provided here, in its attention to teacher development and its specifications related to the three stages of teacher growth (preservice, induction, and inservice), offers an initial conceptualization of a teaching career, one that can be refined over time. Also, the RITE conception of the so-called ideal teacher can provide guidance to decision-makers charged with such difficult tasks as defining and rewarding mastery, and planning for and monitoring organizational schemes that call for teachers to specialize in certain teaching and schooling functions.

Obviously, the RITE framework has as a primary goal the continued professional development of teachers. It would be irrational to suggest that such growth should not have benchmarks and decision points to determine whether teacher development has occurred. Certainly, as our knowledge of teacher growth toward excellence builds, we will be able to be a good deal more precise than we are now. An important research and development agenda is embedded in this declaration, however. As we take more seriously the relationships between teaching expertise, rewards for teachers, the responsibilities of colleges and universities and of school systems to promote teacher growth, and the like, we must systematically accumulate knowledge that will guide us toward clearer specifications of teaching practice at different levels of "mastery," as well as of which teaching functions in a career ladder or differentiated staffing scheme are more valued, and therefore more highly rewarded, than others. It will take concerted, disciplined inquiry and analysis to accomplish these goals.

What is needed is a redefinition of what is to be expected of teachers at different stages of experience and a means to determine the degree to which those expectations are realized by teachers within the stages. Scholars and practitioners need to give their attention to these issues as complementary preoccupations as clinical teacher education moves forward.

TEACHER EVALUATION

Beginning with the description of the "good" or "ideal" teacher presented in Chapter 1 and continuing with characterization of such a teacher at the preservice, induction, and professional stages of teaching, this book has provided information that might be used as a standard against which to compare teacher performance throughout a teaching career. However, we, the authors and the developers of the RITE framework, are concerned about how these depictions of teachers are used. We want to see that the *formative*, developmental view of teacher education that underlies the RITE framework is applied to whatever teacher evaluation is undertaken, whether as part of a RITE clinical teacher education program or in some other teacher education effort. Teacher evaluation that meets these expectations will give particular attention to three aspects of the process.

First, the ongoing, developmental features of the RITE framework will apply. Hence, standards of excellence in teaching will serve as goals for a teacher to attain. Evaluation will emphasize formative purposes and will be used to determine the skills, knowledge, experience, and responsibilities to be acquired or assumed by a teacher, rather than to eliminate teachers from the profession. Different expectations for teacher performance will apply at different stages of a teaching career. Information will be used to delimit next steps in a teacher's development. Staff development programs and other opportunities required to make this advancement will be provided.

As noted above, the descriptions in earlier chapters of the skills, knowledge, and experiences of a proficient teacher at the preservice, induction, and professional career stages provide a starting point for devising such an approach to teacher evaluation. Because these depictions are drawn from both research-based knowledge of effective teaching and the authors' projections of how a RITE-educated teacher will perform, they should be supplemented by inquiry into the appropriateness and effectiveness of the requirements at each career stage and study of the evaluation strategies that are employed. For example, the criteria for the ideal teacher at various stages in a teaching career should be studied to obtain information about factors such as (a) teachers' ability to acquire such knowledge and skills at various points in a teaching career, (b) what occurs when the recommended knowledge and skills are applied in classroom instruction, (c) the knowledge and skills required to support the broadening of the teacher role necessary to a staged career, and (d) the best way to demonstrate that a teacher possesses and effectively uses the various sorts of skill, knowledge, and experience, and fills roles that extend beyond classroom instruction. Thus, at least for the near future, teacher evaluation under the RITE framework should be viewed as a endeavor in *teacher development and research on teaching.*

The second aspect of the RITE framework that warrants special attention for teacher evaluation is self-analysis and reflection. As the reader will recall, one of the key features of RITE clinical teacher education is emphasis upon developmental experiences that require a teacher to obtain information about what takes place in his or her classroom, to analyze this information in terms of what is being accomplished by students, and to reflect upon actions he or she can take to improve the teaching and learning that occur.

Once RITE clinical teacher education becomes an integral part of teacher education within an agency or a consortium of agencies, analysis and reflection by teachers as individuals and as members of peer groups will serve an important evaluation function. The knowledge base regarding adults as learners suggests that information that demonstrates a need for change (improvement) prods an adult to acquire new skills and knowledge. Furthermore, the adult moves to enact the change more readily when he or she acquires this information in a non-threatening manner than when faced with confrontation. Such an evaluation mechanism is provided by self- or peer-initiated and -conducted acquisition and analysis of data and reflection on that analysis, which are an ongoing part of teacher development according to the RITE framework. Recognition of the importance of analysis and reflection as a *formative* tool for evaluation and development at all stages of a teaching career—but particularly the professional (or inservice) stage—is part of the professionalization of teaching.

The third aspect of the RITE framework that is of particular interest for teacher evaluation is the range of teacher capabilities, characteristics, roles, and responsibilities that comprise the "ideal" teacher. The discussion of the ideal teacher in Chapter 1 (p. 4ff.) includes the role of the teacher as a classroom leader and authority figure. It notes the diagnostic and monitoring functions a teacher performs. It underlines the teacher's command of subject matter and of various approaches to delivering it to students. It mentions the ways a teacher interacts with other teachers, parents, and school administrators. It calls for teacher participation in school problem-solving and improvement efforts. The teacher is presented as an inquirer, a learner, and a decision-maker at the classroom, school, and other levels.

Although the RITE framework is limited to the clinical aspects of teaching and teacher education (what occurs in real classrooms and schools), we seek to portray in the above description the full spectrum of a teacher's capabilities, skills, and knowledge outside, as well as inside, the classroom and school. Teacher evaluation, too, should attend to a wide array of both professional capabilities and professional settings.

Unfortunately, the scope of the teacher evaluation approaches and programs presently being initiated first at the state and ultimately at the local school-district levels is at odds with this standpoint of the RITE framework regarding the broad span of expertise used by a professional teacher. In large part, these programs build upon recent research on effective teaching. This research has centered around what occurs in "real" classrooms and, to a lesser extent, "real" schools. Thus, as might be expected, the range of teacher skills and responsibilities included in the evaluation process fall primarily in the "clinical" realm. Moreover, the bulk of attention is given to the teacher-student interaction that occurs in the classroom.

The RITE framework likewise places great importance upon the teacher-student interaction. But within the RITE framework, the ideal teacher also engages in other professional endeavors and utilizes additional types of expertise. As just one example, consider the analytic and reflective feature of the framework mentioned earlier. For a teacher to acquire information, compile this information and extract implications for improvement of instruction, and take actions to alter what occurs in the classroom or school so these improvements can be implemented — all requires important teacher proficiencies. A complete teacher evaluation program would take these skills into account at the preservice and induction stages of teaching and stress them at the professional stage.

Moreover, within the clinical boundaries, differences between "real" classrooms even within "real" schools may demand that a teacher use similar skills and knowledge in different ways, or may require use of entirely different skills, knowledge, and insights depending upon the setting the teacher is in. Extension beyond these settings adds to the complexity of "ideal" teaching and "ideal" teacher evaluation.

Additional examples could be provided of teacher evaluation that incorporates the full range of RITE framework features. This discussion has only touched on the participation of teachers in the evaluation of other teachers. It has only hinted at the purposefulness of the evaluation process and the articulation of these purposes to the teachers being evaluated. It has referenced only once the influence of the context(s) in which a teacher teaches upon what should be evaluated and how the evaluation should be conducted. Nonetheless, the three aspects of teacher evaluation that have been stressed demonstrate that, although not its major purpose, the RITE framework does provide directions for improvement of teacher evaluation. It also offers some directions for further research on teacher evaluation.

ORGANIZATIONAL COLLABORATION

Obviously, the comprehensive view of clinical teacher education provided in this book cannot be implemented by one organization acting independently of others concerned with teacher education. In fact, one of the major problems of educational reform generally and teacher education reform particularly has been and continues to be the uneasy relationships between members of organizations that have common interests.

If one examines the current reform movement, one finds state legislators mandating educational changes that are fought by teacher organizations whose positions are anathema to colleges and universities whose faculty members are ideologically and practically disdainful of much of the teaching and schooling they observe. A specific example of this is in the recent appropriation of research findings as guides to determine first-year teacher competence, a focus of the RITE study of state-mandated teacher induction programs (see Appendix A, Study 3). In this case, the researchers who conducted some of the studies are very uneasy about the use of their findings as competency validation devices. At the same time, teacher education institutions find themselves in the equally uneasy position of having to alter their teacher education programs toward alignment with certification requirements, even in the face of researchers' caveats. Regardless, state and local education officials continue to press forward with their specifications for effective teaching based on what "research says." Clearly, there is a problem here.

What is called for is a dramatic reorientation by educational organizations toward interactive dialogue and decision-making. It is oxymoronic, for example, for teacher preparation programs to become significantly more demanding of students' time (five- or six-year programs) and pocketbooks (an additional five to ten thousand dollars), while state education departments and local school districts maintain low salaries and do little to upgrade teacher status in their regions and communities. *The reform movement in teacher education will probably be judged largely on the basis of the degree to which coalitions of educational organizations can orchestrate the various pieces toward mutually responsive relationships.*

In terms of the clinical teacher education framework presented here, the agenda should be aimed toward common agreement about the nature and purposes of teacher education, the match of program components to expectations for state certification and district conceptions of teaching, and the implementation of reward systems that acknowledge the increased competence of members of the teaching force. This complementarity is difficult to envision, particularly for those of us who have attempted such organizational collaborative efforts. It is, however, the foundation upon which success of the framework and of other important teacher-oriented initiatives rests.

What organizational collaborations will be necessary? At a minimum, implementation of reform in teacher education will require colleges and universities to engage in sustained dialogue with local school agencies and state education departments toward the end of defining in some specific terms what good teaching *is*. It will require that teacher organization members and leaders become less defensive about those within their ranks who might fall outside the conception of good teaching. It will require that state and local boards of education recognize that excellence in teaching, as in any other field, is to a large degree dependent upon the rewards that teaching professionals can earn. This is particularly true in a time when our society is characterized by materialism, and when non-material rewards such as high status in the community are less obvious and less accessible to teachers.

It is only through concerted effort aimed at a comprehensive reformulation of teacher education that the framework proposed herein can achieve its optimum implementation and, we believe, its optimum effect upon the thought, belief, and behavior of teachers. And this effort will require that people of good will, representing heretofore disparate pieces of the educational enterprise, come together toward the realization of common goals for teachers and teaching.

SUPPORT REQUIREMENTS

The previous chapters have included descriptions of how RITE clinical teacher education can be conducted at all stages of a teacher's career. The examples not only incorporate the defining property and the key features of the RITE framework; they also describe practices that change the use of teacher time, particularly the time of more experienced and expert teachers. They illustrate new institutional roles and structures. They suggest new ways to allocate the material and human resources available in universities, colleges, school districts, and schools. They offer reward for and recognition of the experience, skills, and knowledge a teacher acquires and applies as he or she becomes a mature teacher.

Thus, not only is implementation of the key features of the RITE framework essential to effective clinical teacher education, but a maximally effective RITE clinical teacher education program will utilize certain other teacher development resources, structures, and procedures as well. In turn, many of these supporting conditions call for modification in the modus operandi of most educational institutions. Hence, implementation of RITE clinical teacher education will demand the attention of educational administrators, policymakers, and teachers to its support requirements, along with their interest in and concern for application of the RITE framework itself.

For example, consider the use of teacher time that is described in the previous chapters. At the preservice level, experienced teachers are depicted as working with university professors to identify the content of various preservice teacher training courses. Professors and teachers collaborate to build plans for and conduct the clinical aspects of preservice trainees' education. At the induction stage, more experienced and effective teachers become peer coaches, peer observers, model teachers, and helpers for the inductee. Professional teacher education likewise includes use of teachers as peer observers and coaches. In addition, at this stage, teacher participation is expanded to include design of professional development efforts, conduct of training for other experienced teachers, evaluation of the effectiveness of the development efforts engaged in by an individual or group, and study of what occurs when new instructional skills and strategies are applied in the classroom.

Time to engage in such professional activities is central to accomplishment of the participatory and collaborative, developmental, and analytic and reflective roles assigned to teachers in these examples. Adding such involvement to an already full school day obviously is not what the authors had in mind. Nor is it called for by the RITE framework. Rather, policymakers must provide for alternative uses of the hours in the school day.

Teachers who contribute in such professional ways may teach part of a day, and perform other professional functions during the other hours. Or, they may be released from the classroom one day a week to participate in planning meetings, conduct staff development, etc. Other patterns could be suggested. A basic tenet is that excellent teachers should not be entirely removed from contact with students, as they are now, to become preservice student teacher supervisors or inservice staff developers. Their skills and talents should continue to be available to elementary and secondary students part of the time. And members of the teaching profession should have access to their skills and knowledge at other times.

Similar concerns about time apply to teachers who are participating in professional growth and development activities. The purposeful, ongoing, and developmental features of the RITE framework, in particular, call for a drastic reduction in, if not outright elimination of, short-term, all-staff teacher education workshops as the primary mode of staff development for inservice teachers. Thus, it no longer will be appropriate to use after-school hours or a day prior to the start of school as the primary time for teacher development.

As part of the development process, the RITE framework provides for a teacher to inquire into what occurs in his or her classroom, acquire new skills and knowledge over time, apply what is learned, and study what happens when he or she uses new skills and knowledge. Moreover, if teachers are to have opportunities to observe one another, obtain feedback regarding what was observed, and reflect upon what happened, they will need to engage in professional development as well as their instructional roles during the regular school day. For a teacher in the early or middle stages of his or her teaching career, time for such endeavors may not be available on a daily or weekly basis. But it must be available when needed.

These examples of an expanded professional teacher role also entail new institutional roles and structures. Preservice teacher education will involve school-district personnel (such as classroom teachers and perhaps the director of teacher development) in addition to the university staff who typically plan and conduct such training. Teacher development during the induction stage will include university professors as well as teachers and other school-district personnel. Professional teacher development may employ teachers, university professors, and professional associations as well as the staff developers who presently plan and conduct much inservice teacher education. Throughout, teachers will be given new responsibilities; professors, staff developers, and teachers will be asked to share responsibilities that previously were their exclusive domains. Thus, action will be required by multiple institutions.

If educational institutions and the people within them are to share responsibility for career-long development of teachers, and to create the roles and structures necessary to accomplish this goal, purposeful and concerted steps must be taken to encourage such action, as outlined above in the discussion of implementation. The RITE framework will not be fully implemented unless such modifications take place.

The goals of making time available to teachers and establishing new roles and structures lead to questions regarding what allocation of material and human resources will be necessary. To put into practice such ideas as placing professional teachers in the roles of teacher trainers or teacher training program developers will require either additional funds to cover the cost of teachers to work with students when professional teachers are performing these other services, or the redesign of teacher education roles and responsibilities within the university, school district, or school context so available funds can be reallocated to these purposes.

There is no denying that acquisition of additional funds is a challenge for legislators and other policymakers. However, it is relatively clear how such funds could be utilized to support teacher education as required by the RITE framework. On the other hand, reallocation of existing funds presents problems of both acquisition and operations.

Obtaining funds to be reallocated undoubtedly will involve elimination of one or more positions that at present are an accepted part of school-district or university operations. When positions are eliminated, duties and responsibilities associated with those positions must be either eliminated or reassigned. Fortunately, the role of professional teacher defined by the RITE framework can accommodate such change. For example, school-district funds assigned to full-time staff development and curriculum development personnel could be reallocated to obtain time for professional teachers to serve in teacher development or curriculum development roles. As suggested above, expert professional teachers might serve half-time as classroom teachers and half-time in a staff or curriculum development role previously assigned to a full-time non-teacher. There are advantages to such arrangements. No longer would a teacher be expected to do the same thing from year one through year thirty of a career. If the people providing staff development and support services are also teaching, the services they provide will be more apt to be used by teachers. Students will not lose the opportunity to interact with an expert teacher. The list could continue.

At the university level, funds for student teacher supervisor positions, for example, could be reallocated. Professional teachers could be paid to engage in preservice program planning, to conduct seminars and demonstration sessions for teacher candidates, and to supervise the student teachers in their respective classes, and they could be released to supervise other student teachers. Again, this would require important organizational changes. Thus, both the university and the school district would have to do some things differently.

At first glance, the chances of initiating such changes in the ways universities and school districts accomplish their teacher development responsibilities seem dim. However, the influx of new teachers predicted for the decade ahead may provide an impetus for such change. On one hand, the number of new teachers to be prepared may be so large that use of alternative approaches to preservice supervision, for example, may be necessary. On the other hand, due to the difference between the lower salaries paid to new teachers and the salaries of experienced teachers who will retire and be replaced, dollars should be freed for expanding the role and responsibilities of the expert professional teacher, with or without changes in existing staff and curriculum development operations. This "buffer period" should be used by both universities and school districts to test new roles and structures and to identify ways of meeting the support requirements of the RITE framework in terms of time and responsibility that best fit their joint context.

One additional support requirement of the RITE framework warrants attention. This is the importance of establishing ceremonies, rituals, and rewards that recognize and celebrate teachers' growth and development. We have already discussed one powerful mode of recognition: establishing an expanded range of professional activities as part of a professional teaching position, supported by time and money for the conduct of such services. We call for additional attention to the progress from preservice to induction to professional stages of teaching. Opportunities should be provided for teachers to participate in activities previously available primarily to other members of the education profession. For example, attendance at national professional meetings, university colloquia, and state education department "state-of-the-art" seminars would serve the purposes of both recognition and development.

Some forward-looking school districts and universities have provided ideas for creation of such rewards and rituals. One such district holds a banquet to honor all teachers who have successfully completed the induction period of their careers. Civic dignitaries, university dignitaries, and school-district dignitaries attend. The press and other media cover the event. In another district, news reports highlight teachers who are serving in joint university–school-district positions. Yet another district honors and thanks retiring teachers with individual school programs and receptions, and holds a district-wide dinner in their honor. One university school of education holds an afternoon tea to introduce the teachers who will be collaborators for the year in the preservice program to the university faculty. Another university appoints teachers to the advisory board of the school of education.

Such supporting elements will greatly enhance the introduction of RITE clinical teacher education and the advancement of teachers to the level of professional responsibility and expertise the RITE framework aspires to promote. Lack of attention to the requirements for support will reduce the effectiveness of any RITE effort.

CONCLUSION

Clearly, the RITE framework is a complex set of interactive propositions about providing effective clinical teacher education. It is equally clear that the issues that must be dealt with in order to introduce those propositions into reality are equally complex. However, as this chapter has noted, the careful orchestration of a number of variables is necessary to bring to fruition any significant reform in teaching, schooling, and teacher education.

The time is ripe for this reform: The public is expressing concern about the quality of schooling. Members of the education professions are also concerned and, importantly, are expressing their concern in the form of proposals for fundamental change. State and local policymakers are searching for meaningful ways to improve the outcomes of schooling. And the knowledge needed to support the concept of teaching as a profession is increasing rapidly. In these and other sources of ideas for altering the nature of and preparation for teaching there lies enormous potential value for those of us who want to work together toward the improvement of teacher education. The RITE framework is offered as another — and, we believe, a valuable — addition to the important dialogue about changing for the better the educational opportunities available to citizens in our society.

We may not soon again have the set of conditions necessary to bring about a renewal of teaching and the teaching force. We must have the will and the heart to move together toward that renewal.

SYNOPSES OF THREE STUDIES

1

Clinical Teacher Preservice Education

Sharon O'Neal • Susan Barnes • Sara Edwards

PURPOSE

The overall purpose of the Clinical Preservice Teacher Education study was to describe the people, practices, and outcomes of the student teaching experience in two settings, with attention to the characteristics of the participants, their interactions, and the nature of the contexts within which student teaching takes place. The following three questions were addressed:

1. How do the personal, professional, and demographic characteristics of the cooperating teachers, student teachers, and university supervisors impact the student teaching experience?
2. How do the formal and informal institutional contexts influence the student teaching experience?
3. What is the nature of the classroom experience in the preservice clinical setting?

PARTICIPANTS AND SITES

Two universities participated in the study. (Pseudonyms have been used for all participating individuals and institutions to protect their anonymity.) From State University, a large public institution, 44 student teachers, 43 cooperating teachers, and 13 university supervisors participated in this study. From Metropolitan University, a large private institution located in an urban setting, 49 student teachers, 45 cooperating teachers, and 4 university supervisors participated. The total sample therefore consisted of 93 student teachers, 88 cooperating teachers, and 17 university supervisors. Within the sample a subset of 20 student teachers, 20 cooperating teachers, and 9 university supervisors were selected for more intensive examination. Those participants assigned to this group composed the "intensive sample." The remaining cooperating teachers, student teachers, and university supervisors made up the "general sample."

DATA

Whereas quantitative data alone was collected from the general sample, both qualitative and quantitative data were collected from the intensive sample. Data sources included personal journals, audiotapes of conferences and interviews, classroom observations, and university documents as well as various quantitative instruments. These instruments were designed to measure such characteristics as empathy, locus of control, flexibility, self-esteem, conceptual level, cognitive style, vocabulary skills, educational preferences, teacher concerns, and the character of the work life of teachers, among others.

FINDINGS AND CONCLUSIONS

Major findings were classified with regard to participant characteristics, interactions among participants, and the contexts in which these interactions occurred. Conclusions drawn from these aggregate findings are suggested.

Participant Characteristics

Findings. Few site differences were noted in any of the quantitative measures. An analysis of the demographic and background information for each group of participants indicated no significant differences within the groups. In addition, a look at all quantitative data revealed no systematic differences between the general and intensive samples, thus lending generalizability to the findings derived from the in-depth study of the smaller group. The participants did, however, differ by role on a few of the constructs.

Predictably, student teachers were more concerned with other's perceptions of their personal inadequacies than were their more experienced colleagues. For other characteristics there were few differences across role groups; participants reported similarly high self-esteem, high empathy, and progressive educational preference.

On the other hand, cognitive abilities differed according to participant role within the intensive sample. Student teachers scored lowest, cooperating teachers scored in the middle range, and the university supervisors' average scores were the highest.

Conclusions. These data led to the conclusion that, for the most part, within our sample, characteristics were similar not only across settings, but across role groups as well, the most startling difference being on the vocabulary measure. As vocabulary performance can be considered a proxy for general intellectual ability, one could speculate that those entering the teaching force are not as intellectually able as their experienced counterparts. (This conclusion was reinforced when participants reported their high-school standings.)

In sum, participants for the most part were more alike than different. Secondly, the concern expressed in the popular press regarding the deficient abilities of those currently entering the teaching force was partially reinforced by the scores of student teachers on the vocabulary measure.

Context

Findings. Contexts were examined both in terms of the individual schools and classrooms and of the institutions of higher education involved. Student teachers were placed in classrooms which could be characterized in a variety of ways (e.g., low-income, multiple ethnic groups; high-income, predominantly anglo; surburban; urban; etc.). The universities involved in this study varied as well. Whereas one university was a large state-supported institution, the other was a large private university located in an urban area. Perhaps the most interesting difference between the two institutions was at the university supervisor level. Whereas the state university employed graduate students to supervise student teachers as a part-time job, the private institution used individuals with permanent, professional appointments. These appointments at the private institution were funded jointly by the school district involved. In fact, all of these supervisors had "risen from the ranks" of the public school system where they were now supervising student teachers.

Although all cooperating teachers were provided with much information from the universities regarding the student teaching experience, all cooperating teachers reported having received either *not enough* information or *no* information about the general goals, purposes, and requirements of the program.

Regardless of which institution of higher education or public school was involved, all student teachers found comprehensive orientations to their school settings helpful.

Conclusions. Regardless of which participating university or public school was involved, student teaching tended to move along in a similar fashion across all settings. This is especially noteworthy given the differences not only in the schools themselves, but in the training of the university supervisors.

Interactions

Findings. Transcribed conferences showed that cooperating teachers made 72% of the comments during meetings with their student teachers. When student teachers did talk, most of that talk could be characterized as simply acknowledging what their cooperating teacher had said. The topics included, for the most part, discussion of situation-specific issues and their solutions, with little, if any, attention given to a general base of knowledge with regard to teaching. These issues mostly involved specific materials and methodology with little attention given to goals for students or evaluation of classroom students. In addition, conferences contained little, if any, evaluative information directed toward the student teachers. Cooperating teachers did, however, make judgmental remarks about their student teachers in their personal journals. On the other hand, student teachers requested more "constructive criticism."

Student teachers also made evaluative comments about their cooperating teachers in their journals. They spoke of them in a generally positive fashion, using such interpersonal terms as "warm," "loving," "kind," etc. These journal, conference, and interview data not only provide a rich description of the kinds of interactions that took place between cooperating teachers and their student teachers, but reveal that most did not have any set time for planning and conferencing. In fact, no long-range planning was found in one-half of the settings.

Conclusions. Conferences were dominated by cooperating teachers and were characteristic of those held by superiors and subordinates rather than of interactions between professional and beginning professional. Because the content of these conferences focused on situation-specific information about materials and methods, cooperating teachers may have neglected other areas of importance due to the time factor alone. Although student teachers benefited from having many examples to add to their banks of experience, the lack of attention to student goals and evaluation may be a problem when these student teachers move into their own classrooms, which may not be in the same or similar settings.

Cooperating teachers may need guidance not only in providing student teachers with a more generalized knowledge base, but also in skills for evaluating their student teachers. Student teachers reported needing more formative feedback on their weaknesses. Although student teachers *liked* their experiences, often they were unaware of the severity of their weaknesses and thus made no attempt to improve.

In addition, the lack of set planning and conferencing times left student teachers unaware of cooperating teachers' plans until shortly before the student teachers were to teach. Opportunities for in-depth discussion of goals and plans for student progress as well as of day-to-day activities were often not provided.

A complete report of this study may be found in Gary A. Griffin, Susan Barnes, Robert Hughes, Jr., Sharon O'Neal, Maria E. Defino, Sara A. Edwards, and Hobart Hukill, *Clinical Preservice Teacher Education: Final Report of a Descriptive Study*, Report No. 9025 (Austin, TX: The University of Texas at Austin, Research and Development Center for Teacher Education, 1983).

2

Changing Teacher Practice:
An Experimental Study of Inservice
Clinical Teacher Education

Sara Edwards • Susan Barnes

This study was an attempt to develop a link between research findings and potential users. The research findings came from studies of effective teaching and studies of change. These two bodies of research findings were integrated in an intervention strategy aimed at causing effective staff developer behaviors, effective teaching, and ultimately, positive pupil outcomes. The targeted potential users were persons responsible for building-level staff development in a school district. The study used findings from research on teaching as content for a planned intervention, and research on teacher and school change as the basis for a delivery system for that content. These two bodies of information were combined into a specific change strategy, which was introduced to staff development personnel in an ongoing school setting. Participants were observed for treatment effects on staff developer behaviors, teacher behaviors, and on-task student behaviors.

141

THE INTERVENTION

The teacher behaviors forming the content of the inservice training have been identified in the line of research generally referred to as "teacher effectiveness research." An operational definition of the effective teacher emerged from this line of research: The effective teacher is the teacher whose classes regularly score higher on standardized achievement tests than do classes of other teachers, after entering differences between classes are statistically controlled. Specific behaviors were grouped into the following categories.

The "Effective" Teacher

1. Plans and prepares for class.
2. Actively presents the lesson.
3. Interacts with students in situationally appropriate manner.
4. Conducts practice over new material.
5. Monitors seatwork.
6. Holds students responsible for assignments.
7. Plans rules and procedures.
8. Actively presents rules and procedures.
9. Holds students responsible for behavior.
10. Reacts to students' behavior consistently.

Although there are other conceptions of good teaching that view teaching as an art or as a job requiring certain philosophical or psychological orientations, the Changing Teacher Practice study was concerned only with recent findings in classroom-based research, and not with the assumptions underlying this particular approach to the study of teaching.

A set of research-based conclusions about school change guided this effort. These conclusions, more often than not, emerged as a consequence of post hoc analyses of efforts at innovation in schools. One principal finding of change-oriented research is that attempts to change are often situation-specific. That is, the contexts in which the change efforts take place vary widely, and the variation appears to produce equally variable effects unless the change strategy accounts for such variance in contexts. Therefore, the Changing Teacher Practice intervention deliberately had as a component the opportunity for staff developers to select strategies and teaching behaviors that, after systematic reflection about situation-specific school variables, fitted their settings. The intervention was implemented such that the conclusions from the change literature were consciously attended to, while at the same time staff development personnel made the primary, situation-specific decisions about how to move forward with the change strategy.

The strategy proposed a set of options for working with teachers and focused participants' attention on the need to make reasoned and rational selections from the set. Staff developers were not required to focus on any or all of the research-derived teaching behaviors, but were encouraged to select the ones that were most appropriate for the teachers with whom they worked. This strategy was based on the assumption that school leaders can provide instructional leadership to faculty groups if they are helped to focus their behavior and if they have a knowledge base from which they can work.

The research on the process of change provides a description of various practices that have been found to be positively associated with the successful implementation of innovations. This research also provides conceptualizations of instructional leadership and teaching that are coherent and that could serve as rallying points around which to organize practice. For the RITE study, this research was translated from the sometimes painful jargon of the research community into the more conventional language of schools. This translation was accomplished in some instances in print, by the resource materials provided to participants, and in others interpersonally, by the RITE research team during the intervention. The strategy was conceptually and practically linked to ongoing processes and expectations in the school setting. The demand of the strategy was to consider and act upon the perceived match between school/classroom characteristics and a set of research-based options for leadership and teaching practice.

These broad areas of leader behavior were more sharply defined in operational terms and presented as part of the Changing Teacher Practice intervention in the form of a list of desired staff developer behaviors. This descriptive listing is neither exhaustive nor absolute, but it is logically generalizable and predictable in terms of expected results.

Successful Staff Developer Practices

1. Focus on teacher behaviors.
2. Identify specific, concrete resources and available technical assistance.
3. Provide teachers with opportunities to interact with one another about teaching and schooling.
4. Provide teachers with opportunities to observe one another and to discuss what was observed.
5. Provide teachers with opportunities to plan together.
6. Provide teachers with opportunities to implement their plans.
7. Diagnose school- and classroom-specific regularities.
8. Diagnose individual stages of concern of teachers.
9. Attend to school and classroom regularities and teachers' concerns in formulating inservice activities.
10. Include the building administrator in activities designed to help teachers be more effective.
11. Work with teachers on adaptation of teaching strategies ac-

cording to the characteristics of students, the classroom, and the school.

12. Provide in-classroom technical assistance (e.g., coaching) to teachers.
13. Link teachers to technical assistance outside the immediate school environment and provide concrete resources.
14. Provide teachers with feedback which is objective, concrete, and focused.
15. Provide consistent, ongoing assistance to teachers.
16. Adapt staff development behavior according to personal and organizational characteristics of "users."
17. Use teacher time to deal with teacher problems, issues, and concerns.
18. Communicate expectations clearly and precisely.
19. Interact with teachers in friendly and positive ways.
20. Provide teachers with evidence that "teachers can make a difference" in pupil outcomes.
21. Demonstrate knowledge of "effective" teaching as revealed by research.
22. Engage teachers in problem identification, solution formulation, and testing activities.
23. Reflect upon the effects of one's behavior and use that reflection as a basis for decisions about maintenance or modification of that behavior.

SAMPLE

A treatment group–control group quasi-experimental design was used to assess the impact of this intervention. A representative group was selected, consisting of 10 persons who were responsible for working with teachers in an effort to promote more effective teaching and school improvement in the selected district. These 10 teacher developers were assigned to five pairs, matched as closely as possible according to role, socioeconomic status of the school, prior experience, years in the position, and reputation for effectiveness. One of each pair was randomly assigned to the treatment group, and one to the control group. Each staff developer selected two teachers from among the group with whom he or she worked. Those 10 teachers working with the staff developer treatment group constituted the teacher treatment group, and the other 10 constituted the teacher control group. Students of the treatment group teachers constituted the treatment group students. Students of control group teachers constituted the control group students.

FINDINGS AND CONCLUSIONS

Treatment group staff developers demonstrated slightly more than twice as many of the desired staff developer behaviors as did the control group. The results of a Mann-Whitney test indicate that this difference is statistically significant at the .01 level. The within-group means were also in favor of the treatment group, in that the highest mean for the control group was lower than the lowest mean for the treatment group.

What seems to have happened with the treatment group staff developers is that they used the relatively unconventional leadership behaviors (e.g., adaptation of their own behaviors to fit their teachers, provision of technical assistance outside the school, provision of opportunities for teachers to interact and plan together, etc.), and focused those behaviors on teaching. The finding that there was such a dramatic difference between treatment and control staff developers in terms of focusing on teaching supports the possibility that the Changing Teacher Practice intervention provided school leaders with a body of knowledge about classroom life that was coherent, organized, and, one suspects, meaningful to teachers.

The intervention used with the staff developers affected the teaching behaviors of the treatment group teachers in the desired direction. The greatest differences in teaching effects were seen in two important components of the teaching process: planning and presenting. These differences were seen whether the content of that teaching process was academic or involved rules and procedures for classroom activity.

Practitioners in this study were neither disdainful of nor resistant to lessons learned from systematic inquiry. Although the study did not specifically address this issue, participant self-reports at the conclusion of the study testified to its importance in their decisions to adopt the strategy in schools and classrooms.

In sum, the implementation of the Changing Teacher Practice strategy in terms of practice suggests that similar interventions will be positively viewed and acted upon when research is seen as directly related to the problems and issues in the setting, is relatively familiar to participants in terms of practical activity, is understandable conceptually and linguistically, and is subject to adaptation depending upon the character of the setting. Findings from this deliberate attempt to bridge the gap between research and potential users suggest that under these conditions practitioners will use the results of research.

When the study was completed and the findings were available, the district adopted the Changing Teacher Practice intervention for 175 elementary and middle-school principals and resource teachers.

A complete report of this study may be found in Gary A. Griffin, Susan Barnes, Sharon O'Neal, Sara A. Edwards, Maria E. Defino, and Hobart Hukill, *Changing Teacher Practice: Final Report of an Experimental Study*, Report No. 9052 (Austin, TX: The University of Texas at Austin, Research and Development Center for Teacher Education, 1984).

A Study of State-Mandated Beginning Teacher Programs and Their Effects

James Hoffman • Sharon O'Neal • Margaret Paulissen

The purpose of this research was to describe how certain state-mandated induction programs affected the transition from student of teaching to teacher. Areas of focus included program intents, critical program features, implementation processes, and program effects.

THE SAMPLE

The programs included in this study were identified through an exhaustive review process. First, program descriptions from the four states with operational teacher induction programs were solicited and reviewed. Resource limitations, coupled with a desire to develop a rich qualitative data base for the study, necessitated a focus on just two of these four states. The final determination of the two states included in the RITE sample was based in part on geographical spread, in part on an informal survey of teacher educators designed to identify "promising" programs in the country, and in part on whether explicit attention to both assistance and assessment dimensions was found in the materials describing each program.

The induction program in State #1 was mandated by one component of a more comprehensive House Bill passed in 1980. The declared intent of the legislation was to establish qualifications for teachers to ensure that the education of children would be provided by teachers of demonstrated ability. In State #1, the department of education developed a standard plan of implementation that is being used statewide including time lines and report forms. The district bears responsibility for establishing an assistance/assessment committee to work with each new teacher. According to the state guidelines, the committee must include an experienced teacher, a building level administrator, and one other educator from an institution of higher education. This committee has the responsibility to observe the new teacher in the classroom and to meet with the new teacher to offer assistance. An observation instrument focusing on four "categories" (human relations, teaching and assessment, classroom management, and professionalism) is used. This committee makes the recommendation regarding certification for the new teacher.

The induction program in State #2 was mandated through a Senate Bill approved in 1981 which provided for a beginning teacher program. The purposes of this program were to: (1) increase student learning by providing a set of supervised support services for teachers in their first year(s) of teaching in the state that would assist them in their continuing professional development, and (2) meet the requirements of the state statute and administrative code. Successful completion of the program is required for the superintendent or chief administrator to recommend the teacher for a full certificate. A State Board Rule in State #2 effective July 1, 1982, defined the Beginning Teacher Program as a "formal" program of at least one year. Each school district was required to submit a plan for approval by May 1, 1982. The state's guidelines specified the components to be included, but each school district was responsible for developing its own specific plan and submitting that plan to the state board for approval. This plan had to include provision for supervised support services for the continuing development and demonstration of specified competencies by the new teacher. The beginning teacher support staff must include a peer teacher, a building-level administrator, and one other (professional) educator. A "summative" evaluation plan must be provided that includes observation instruments and evaluation procedures to demonstrate successful performance of the minimum essential competencies. At least two summative evaluations are required, one within 90 working days of the beginning of the employment period in order to provide assistance where observations suggest it is needed. At least three "formative" conferences are required, and each conference is based on at least one observation by a support team member using a set of common criteria. The state has developed and validated an observation instrument that can be used for this purpose. The instrument targets teaching behaviors in six domains: (1) planning, (2) management of student contact, (3) instructional organization and development, (4) presentation of subject matter, (5) communication, verbal and non-verbal, and (6) evaluation. Individual districts are free to propose an alternative to the state-developed instrument, provided they can demonstrate stringent reliability characteristics and meet criteria for validity in the essential competency areas.

Two districts within each targeted state were identified based on nominations for excellence in educational programming made by leaders in the state educational system and selected university-based teacher educators. The rationale for this sampling strategy was the goal of studying the implementation and effects of induction programs under optimal conditions. All four districts included in our sample from these two states were in their second year of implementation of the program at the time of the RITE study. In State #2, both districts were using the state-developed assessment instrument.

Sixteen beginning teachers were drawn from the four districts in the sample. In each district, two of the beginning teachers were to have been teaching in the same elementary school, and the other two in the same junior high or senior high school. Working cooperatively with district-level administrators, we were successful in gaining commitments from four beginning teachers in each district (two elementary and two junior high/secondary), although the actual school assignments within districts were not balanced in the manner we had intended. In only three cases did we have two beginning teachers in the same school setting. The members of each beginning teacher's support team were invited to participate in the study. Only one person (the peer teacher on a beginning teacher's team in State #2) declined to participate.

DATA COLLECTION AND ANALYSIS

We drew on numerous data sources in the process of conducting this study. Each beginning teacher participated in six interviews with RITE staff spaced throughout the year and completed a series of inventories and questionnaires. Beginning teachers were also observed on six occasions by RITE staff. Extensive data were also collected from the support team members. The focus in this data collection was on documenting: support team member activity in the program, impressions and evaluations of the beginning teacher, impressions and evaluations of program features, and personal impact as a result of participation. Peer teachers were interviewed and observed on at least three occasions. They maintained journals and completed essentially the same battery of inventories and questionnaires as the beginning teachers. The building-level administrators and "other educators" were interviewed on three occasions, maintained journals, and completed the Hunt's Paragraph Completion Test. Finally, program directors at the district level were interviewed three times during the year. The principle focus for these interviews was on program implementation.

The primary approach to data reduction and analysis was qualitative and focused on two areas: program implementation and program effects. All data sources were scrutinized and, to the degree possible, triangulated in an effort to gather valid data on these areas. Four district-level profiles and sixteen case studies (one for each beginning teacher's experience in the program) were constructed in this manner.

FINDINGS AND DISCUSSION

Program Implementation

Leadership in each district was vested in a program director. All four program directors were articulate in describing program intents and features. Our analyses confirmed implementation of the beginning teacher programs in each of the four districts with "high fidelity" to the broad state mandates and locally adopted provisions. Throughout the course of interviews spaced over the year, the program directors also demonstrated ongoing awareness of the progress of the beginning teachers included in our sample, even though these teachers represented only four of the many first-year teachers in each district. The only two problem areas that surfaced at the district level were with respect to "getting started" and support team assignments.

At the school level, our analyses of implementation revealed that substantive implementation was uneventful across school sites and seemed to be associated more often than not with two factors: (1) strong team leadership, and/or (2) prior contact. The "formal" leadership role was most often assumed by the building-level administrator, but in some cases the other educator took on this responsibility. In cases where no strong team leadership appeared, the induction program seldom rose above the procedural compliance level. Where there had been prior contact with the school by the beginning teacher (in particular through student teaching in the same setting), substantive implementation seemed to be at its greatest. Six of the sixteen beginning teachers in our sample had completed student teaching in the school to which they were assigned for their first year of teaching. In all of these cases the enactment of the program was accomplished with ease and enthusiasm. There was an active commitment on the part of team members to seeing the first-year teacher through this experience successfully.

Program Impact

In reporting on program impact we will rely primarily, but not exclusively, on data reflecting the participants' perceptions of program impact.

Beginning teachers. The first year of teaching was not regarded as easy by the majority of beginning teachers in our sample. The kinds of concerns of beginning teachers uncovered in other studies, such as concerns about self (e.g., Do I fit? . . . Am I adequate as a classroom teacher? . . .) and concerns about task (e.g., classroom management, content coverage), were well represented in our sample. Still, the experience was not as traumatic or incapacitating as some have argued. Rather, for the majority of beginning teachers, the first year was a demanding but manageable experience not without its rewards. The vast majority of our teachers felt the year had been a positive growing experience, and all but two expressed the desire to return the following year.

As far as the impact of the induction programs, at their worst, the programs represented one more set of things to deal with in addition to the demands typically facing the first-year teacher. For a small number of our beginning teachers, the program seemed to heighten anxiety and uncertainty about their expectations for success. This was particularly true at the beginning of the year, when the first-year teachers were unclear about the exact nature of the program and its potential consequences for them personally. As the year passed and these few teachers gained a better understanding of the program, anxiety and uncertainty turned to apathy and sometimes hostility toward the program. The shift was most apparent in relation to the assessment or evaluation components of the programs. Our data indicated a strong shift in perception among first-year teachers of the importance of the evaluation procedures used, from the early part of the year to the end. At the beginning of the year there appeared to be a strong feeling that these evaluation procedures were very influential on their behavior. By the end of the year the rating of importance dropped precipitously.

At their best, these programs assured early and sometimes frequent contact between the beginning teachers and "significant others" in the educational context in which they found themselves. This description fits the majority of the first-year teachers in our sample. For most of our beginning teachers, the most significant positive force on their experience was the peer or support teacher. The peer or support teacher was rated as extremely influential early in the year and continued to grow in influence as the year progressed. Peer/support teachers were regarded and referred to by beginning teachers variously as mentors, counselors, friends, and colleagues. They were valued primarily as a source of practical information and secondarily as a source of psychological support. Contacts with principals and other educators, though less frequent, were noted by many of the beginning teachers as being important influences on their first year of teaching. The contacts with the principal through the program (when positive in nature) were interpreted and valued by the beginning teachers as approval and acceptance by the primary authority figure in the school. The "other educator" seemed to have the least impact on most teams, but was still rated as an important contributor by most of the first-year teachers. In State #1 (where the other educators were drawn from higher education), the comments of the first-year teachers reflected the feeling that the approval of the other educator of their teaching performance was a continuing affirmation of their success and growth from the preservice experience.

The programs not only provided that contact occurred, but via the prescribed assessment procedures ensured that the focal point for the contacts was the activity of teaching (insofar as teaching is represented in the assessment devices). The language used to describe teacher strengths and areas of need reflected the terminology used in the systems designed to evaluate performance.

These comments should not be taken to mean that all first-year teachers in our sample were impacted to the same degree or even in a positive manner. Four of the first-year teachers in our sample were dissatisfied with the program and questioned its value. Three of the four dissatisfied teachers were from the junior high/secondary level. All three were in difficult situations in terms of teaching load (anywhere from four to five course preparations per day), and all three had significant teaching responsibilities in areas outside their specialized fields. The fourth dissatisfied teacher was trained in physical education at the secondary level, but was teaching at the elementary level.

The support team. The program "intents" as revealed through legislative acts and program descriptions do not specify impact on program participants other than the first-year teachers and their students. It became clear to us, however, as we analyzed the case data, that many of the other participants were affected by their work in the program. Many of the support teachers, while reporting that they had often "helped" or taken first-year teachers under their wings in the past, indicated that this program made the contact different. The recognition and responsibility that accompanied their participation gave them an enhanced image of themselves as professionals. Many of the principals, in particular those in State #2, were positive about learning the assessment instrument used in this program. The extensive training provided to principals in the use of this instrument was found to be useful to them in their observations of regular teachers in their schools. They were pleased to find a research-based instrument that specified effective teaching behaviors. Many of the "other educators" (the university-based team members) from State #1 reported that the contact with the schools was a growing experience for them. Many commented on how observing graduates of their own programs functioning in real classrooms forced them to reflect on their treatment of preservice teachers.

The only significant (consistent) negative impact statements came from building-level administrators who voiced concerns over the amount of paper work required by the program, in particular in those cases where the outcome (in terms of a positive recommendation for a first-year teacher) was clear from the beginning. This concern was even more pronounced where there were many first-year teachers at a single campus site.

Fulfillment of State (Policy) Intents

The four district-level directors were positive about their programs and indicated that this positive view was shared by most educators in their districts. The directors expressed greatest satisfaction with the assistance and support being provided to the first-year teachers through the induction programs. Most of the directors expressed the view at one point or another that the degree of success in this "assistance" function was tied to the effectiveness of the individual first-year teacher's support team.

Although satisfaction was expressed in most cases with the "mechanics" of assessment, there was some concern over whether the program was effective in screening the profession. This observation takes on heightened significance when we consider that all of the teachers included in our sample and practically all of the first-year teachers in the four districts were recommended for certification. Of course, it is possible that by virtue of our focus on highly regarded districts, we had isolated in our sample a group of promising first-year teachers. Indeed, the data from our own observations documented the use of effective teaching behaviors by these first-year teachers at levels comparable to those of experienced teachers observed in other studies. Such performance would place all of the teachers we studied well above the minimal levels represented in the assessment devices. On the other hand, additional data secured through interviews with state officials indicated that nearly all of the teachers enrolled in the programs in the two states were recommended for certification. Such patterns would seem to call into question either the "gatekeeping" capacity of such programs or the real need for such programs in the first place if justified on the grounds of controlling for quality of entering teachers.

A complete report of this study can be found in James V. Hoffman, Gary A. Griffin, Sara A. Edwards, Margaret O. Paulissen, Sharon F. O'Neal, Susan Barnes, and Deborah A. Verstegen, *Teacher Induction Study: Final Report of a Descriptive Study* (Austin, TX: The University of Texas at Austin, Research and Development Center for Teacher Education, 1985).

Appendix B

COLLOQUIA AND PARTICIPANTS

1

EFFECTIVE CLINICAL TEACHER EDUCATION: INSERVICE LEVEL

April 19, 1985 • Santa Barbara, CA

FRANCES HAYWOOD
Woodland Hills, California

LAURENCE IANNACCONE
Santa Barbara, California

MICHAEL MCKIBBIN
Sacramento, California

STEVE KINGSFORD
Ventura, California

MICHAEL KLENTSCHY
Los Angeles, California

NANCY LAURSEN
La Puente, California

CAROL LEIGHTY
San Diego, California

THOMAS PEELER
Santa Barbara, California

2

EFFECTIVE CLINICAL TEACHER EDUCATION: INDUCTION LEVEL
May 3, 1985 • Falls Church, VA

JOHNNIE HAMILTON
Springfield, Virginia

VIRGINIA KOEHLER
College Park, Maryland

FRANK LYMAN
Columbia, Maryland

JIM PATTON
Richmond, Virginia

DIANA SCHMELZER
Southlakes, Virginia

TERRY WILDMAN
Blacksburg, Virginia

3

EFFECTIVE CLINICAL TEACHER EDUCATION: PRESERVICE LEVEL

May 17, 1985 • Chicago, IL

JANE ALLEN
Wilmette, Illinois

ESTELLE FAULK
Chicago, Illinois

ROBERT FISHER
Normal, Illinois

JOHN MCDONNEL
Beloit Wisconsin

ETHEL MIGRA
Evanston, Illinois

SAM YARGER
Milwaukee, Wisconsin

Notes

NOTES TO FOREWORD

1. Virginia R. Koehler, "Research on Preservice Teacher Education," *Journal of Teacher Education* 36, no. 1 (1985): 23–30.
2. Walter Doyle, "Learning to Teach: An Emerging Direction in Research on Preservice Teacher Education," *Journal of Teacher Education* 36, no. 1 (1985): 31–33.
3. Judith Warren Little, "Norms of Collegiality and Experimentation: Workplace Conditions of School Success," *American Education Research Journal* 19, no. 3 (1982): 325–340.
4. Judith Warren Little, "Teachers as Colleagues," in Virginia R. Koehler, ed., *The Educator's Handbook: Research into Practice* (New York: Longman, Inc., in press).
5. Gary A. Griffin, Susan Barnes, Robert Hughes, Jr., Sharon O'Neal, Maria E. Defino, Sara A. Edwards, and Hobart Hukill, *Clinical Preservice Teacher Education: Final Report of a Descriptive Study*, Report No. 9025 (Austin, TX: The University of Texas at Austin, Research and Development Center for Teacher Education, 1983).

NOTES TO CHAPTER 1

1. Barak Rosenshine, "Teaching Functions in Instructional Programs," *The Elementary School Journal* 83 (March 1983): 335–352.
2. Maxine Greene, *Landscapes of Learning* (New York: Teachers College Press, 1978).
3. Elliot Eisner, *The Educational Imagination: On the Design and Evaluation of School Programs* (New York: Macmillan Publishing Company, 1985).
4. George S. Counts, "Dare Schools Build a New Social Order?" *John Day Pamphlets*, 26 (1932).
5. This conceptualization is demonstrated in a special issue of the *Journal of Teacher Education* that presents papers prepared for a national conference on teacher education held at the Research and Development Center for Teacher Education at The University of Texas at Austin, Austin, Texas, in October, 1984. *Journal of Teacher Education* 36, No. 1 (January-February 1985).

6. Judith E. Lanier, "Tensions in Teaching Teachers the Skills of Pedagogy," in Gary A. Griffin, ed., *Staff Development*, Eighty-second Yearbook of the Society for the Study of Education (Chicago: University of Chicago Press, 1983), 118–153.

7. John I. Goodlad, *A Place Called School* (New York: McGraw-Hill Company, 1983).

8. Gary A. Griffin and Hobart Hukill, *Alternate Perspectives for Research and Development in Teacher Education*, Report No. 9019 (Austin, TX: The University of Texas at Austin, Research and Development Center for Teacher Education, 1982).

9. Gary A. Griffin, Ann Lieberman, and Joann Jacullo-Noto, *Interactive Research and Development on Schooling: Final Report* (New York: Teachers College, Columbia University, 1982).

10. Gary A. Griffin, Susan Barnes, Robert Hughes, Jr., Sharon O'Neal, Maria E. Defino, Sara A. Edwards, and Hobart Hukill, *Clinical Preservice Teacher Education: Final Report of a Descriptive Study*, Report No. 9025 (Austin, TX: The University of Texas at Austin, Research and Development Center for Teacher Education, 1983).

11. Gary A. Griffin, Susan Barnes, Sharon O'Neal, Sara A. Edwards, Maria E. Defino, and Hobart Hukill, *Changing Teacher Practice: Final Report of an Experimental Study* (Austin, TX: The University of Texas at Austin, Research and Development Center for Teacher Education, 1984).

12. Sara A. Edwards and Sharon O'Neal, "Implementing New Teacher Programs in Classrooms" (Paper presented at the Annual Meeting of the American Educational Research Association, Chicago, 1985).

13. See, for example, William J. Tikunoff, Beatrice A. Ward, and Gary A. Griffin, *Interactive Research and Development on Teaching: Final Report* (San Francisco, CA: Far West Laboratory for Educational Research and Development, 1979); Judith Warren Little, *School Success and Staff Development: The Role of Staff Developer in Urban Desegregated Schools* (Boulder, CO: Center for Action Research, 1982); Paul Berman and Milbrey W. McLaughlin, *Federal Programs Supporting Education Change*, Vol. 4 (Santa Monica, CA: Rand, 1975); Stewart C. Purkey and Marshall S. Smith, "Effective Schools: A Review," *The Elementary School Journal* 83, No. 4 (1983): 427–452; M. Maxine Bentzen, *Changing Schools: The Magic Feather Principle* (New York: McGraw-Hill Book Company, 1974); Griffin, Lieberman, and Jacullo-Noto, *Interactive Research and Development on Schooling*.

14. Much of the conception of the good teacher presented here is derived from Gary A. Griffin, "Research in Preservice Teacher Education" (Paper presented at the NIE Research into Practice Conference, Detroit, 1982).

15. James V. Hoffman and Maria E. Defino, "State and School District Intentions and the Implementation of New Teacher Programs" (Paper presented at the Annual Meeting of the American Educational Research Association, Chicago, 1985).

16. Elliot G. Mishler, "Meaning in Context: Is There Any Other Kind?" *Harvard Educational Review* 49, no. 1: 1–19.

17. Beatrice A. Ward and William J. Tikunoff, "Why Consider Context?" (Paper presented at the Annual Meeting of the American Educational Research Association, New York, 1977).

18. Gary A. Griffin, "Thinking about Teaching," in Karen K. Zumwalt, ed., *Yearbook of the Association of Supervision and Curriculum Development* (Alexandria, VA: The Association, in press).

19. Tikunoff, Ward, and Griffin, *Interactive Research and Development: Final Report*.

20. See Sara A. Edwards, *Clinical Preservice Activities: Education, Development, Training— Three Case Studies* (Austin, TX: The University of Texas at Austin, Research and Development Center for Teacher Education, 1982); Susan Barnes and Sara A. Edwards, *Effective Student Teaching Experience: A Qualitative-Quantitative Study* (Austin, TX: The University of Texas at Austin, Research and Development Center for Teacher Education, 1984).

21. Matthew B. Miles, ed., *Innovation in Education* (New York: Teachers College, Columbia University, 1964).

22. Griffin et al., *Clinical Preservice Teacher Education: Final Report of a Descriptive Study*.

23. Griffin et al., *Changing Teacher Practice: Final Report of an Experimental Study*.

24. Edwards and O'Neal, "Implementing New Teacher Programs."
25. In fact, just such a general statement guided the implementation of the Interactive Research and Development projects already cited. Although there were some restrictions placed upon *how* investigations might be carried forward, in terms of research requirements, *what* was to be investigated was open to team members.
26. This was true for a number of the cooperating teachers in the RITE study of student teaching. It is not claimed here that these teachers never knew the purposes, or even that they were not presented with information about expectations and role definitions. What is claimed is that the teachers, upon direct questioning, could not respond such that issues of purpose were clearly defined.
27. Griffin et al., *Changing Teacher Practice: Final Report of an Experimental Study.*
28. Edwards and O'Neal, "Implementing New Teacher Programs."
29. Ann Lieberman, "Educational Policy and Leadership" (Paper presented at the Allerton Symposium on Institutional Collaboration, Monticello, IL, 1985).
30. Gary A. Griffin and Sara A. Edwards, *Student Teaching: Problems and Promising Practices,* Report No. 9015 (Austin, TX: The University of Texas at Austin, Research and Development Center for Teacher Education, 1982).
31. Judith Warren Little, *School Success and Staff Development.*
32. Grant Behnke, Janice Bennett, Cindy Chase, Jane Day, Charlotte Lazar, and David Mittleholtz, "Coping with Classroom Distractions," *Elementary School Journal* 81, no. 3 (1981): 135–155.
33. Gary A. Griffin, "Toward a Conceptual Framework for Staff Development," in Gary A. Griffin, ed., *Staff Development,* Eighty-second Yearbook of the National Society for the Study of Education (Chicago, IL: The University of Chicago Press, 1983).
34. Gary A. Griffin, "The Paraprofessionalization of Teaching" (Paper presented at the Annual Meeting of the American Educational Research Association, Chicago, 1985).
35. Griffin et al., *Clinical Preservice Teacher Education: Final Report of a Descriptive Study.*
36. Ann Lieberman and Lynne Miller, *Staff Development: New Demands, New Realities, New Perspectives* (New York: Teachers College Press, 1978).
37. Maxine Greene, "How Do We Think About Our Craft?" *Teachers College Record* 86, no. 1 (1984).
38. Willis D. Hawley, Susan J. Rosenholtz, Henry Goodstein, and Ted Hasselbrign, *Good Schools: What Research Says About Improving Student Achievement* (Nashville, TN: Vanderbilt University, 1984).
39. Gary A. Griffin, "New Teacher Programs and Certification: Conclusions, Questions, and Speculations" (Paper presented at the annual meeting of the American Educational Research Association, Chicago, 1985).
40. In the RITE study of student teaching, for example, the general view held by many cooperating teachers was that the student teachers' so-called "theory" needed to be "unlearned" during student teaching. Not only was "theory" a misunderstood term, but it was considered largely negative in terms of promoting classroom effectiveness. Clearly, for these teachers, the power of theory as both explanation and prediction had not been demonstrated to be relevant to their conceptions of teaching.
41. *Teachers College Record* 86, No. 1 (1984): entire issue.
42. *Beginning Teacher Induction — Five Dilemmas: Proceedings from a Public Forum* (Austin, TX: The University of Texas at Austin, Research and Development Center for Teacher Education, 1982).
43. Frances F. Fuller and Oliver Bown, "Becoming a Teacher," in Kevin Ryan, ed., *Teacher Education,* Seventy-fourth Yearbook of the National Society for the Study of Education (Chicago: University of Chicago Press, 1975).
44. Bruce Joyce and Renee Clift, "The Phoenix Agenda: Essential Reform in Teacher Education," *Educational Researcher* 13, no. 4 (1984): 5–18.
45. Despite some initial skepticism, it is clear that the report of the National Commission on Ex-

cellence in Education sparked widespread public interest in the issues related to providing quality education. The theme of "excellence" as a goal for schooling was picked up by the National Commission for Excellence in Teacher Education. It is too early to determine the influence of this latter report.

46. Norman A. Sprinthall and Lois Thies-Sprinthall, "The Teacher as an Adult Learner: A Cognitive-Developmental View," in Gary A. Griffin, ed., *Staff Development*, Eighty-second Yearbook of the National Society for the Study of Education (Chicago: University of Chicago Press, 1983).

47. Fuller and Bown, "Becoming a Teacher."

48. Phillip C. Schlechty, *Teaching as a Profession: What We Know and What We Need to Know about Teachers* (Paper presented at the Annual Meeting of the American Educational Research Association, Chicago, 1985).

49. The entire issue of *The Elementary School Journal*, Fall, 1985, is devoted to discussions of the concept of the master teacher.

50. The idea of career stages for teachers has captured the imagination of a number of legislators, lay persons, and educators. Generally, this idea takes the form of a recommendation that teachers move through such stages as novice, beginning teacher, career teacher, and professional career teacher. In such a progression, responsibilities and rewards would be differentiated according to the roles played by teachers at various career stages. This is seen as a way both to attract teachers to the profession because of the promise of greater reward, and to hold teachers in the profession because of increased professional responsibility.

51. Lieberman and Miller, *Staff Development*.

52. Tikunoff, Ward, and Griffin, *Interactive Research and Development on Teaching: Final Report*.

53. Gary A. Griffin, "Why Use Research in Preservice Teacher Education: A Proposal," *Journal of Teacher Education* 35, no. 4 (1984): 36-40.

54. John Dewey, *Democracy and Education* (Toronto: Macmillan Company, 1944).

55. Susan Barnes and Sara A. Edwards, *Effective Student Teaching Experience: A Qualitative-Quantitative Study*.

56. The National Commission on Excellence in Education, *A Nation at Risk: The Imperative for Educational Reform* (Washington, DC: U.S. Government Printing Office, 1983).

NOTES TO CHAPTER 2

1. For a more extended discussion of the notion of "novice teachers," see Sharon Feiman-Nemser, "Learning to Teach," in Lee S. Shulman and Gary Sykes (eds.), *Handbook of Teaching and Policy* (New York: Longman, Inc., 1983).

2. Jane H. Applegate and Thomas J. Lasley, "What Cooperating Teachers Expect from Preservice Field Experience Students," *Teacher Education* 24 (1984): 70-82.

3. Bruce Joyce and Renee Clift, "The Phoenix Agenda: Essential Reform in Teacher Education," *Educational Researcher* 13, no. 4 (1984): 5-18.

4. The term *predisposition* is here intended to reflect on attitude or, as Rokeach puts its, ". . . a relatively enduring organization of beliefs around an object or situation predisposing one to respond in some preferential manner." See Milton Rokeach, *Beliefs, Attitudes and Values: A Theory of Organization and Change* (San Francisco: Jossey & Bass, 1968).

5. Willis D. Copeland, "Processes Mediating the Relationship Between Cooperating Teacher Behavior and Student Teacher Classroom Performance," *Journal of Educational Psychology* 70, no. 1 (1978): 95-100.

6. Kenneth Howey, Sam A. Yarger, and Bruce Joyce, *Inservice Teacher Education* (Washington, DC: Association of Teacher Education, 1979).

7. Susan Barnes and Sara A. Edwards, *Effective Student Teaching Experience: A Qualitative-Quantitative Study* (Austin, TX: The University of Texas at Austin, Research and Development Center for Teacher Education, 1984).

8. Carolyn M. Bogad, "Recruitment and Socialization as Recurring Issues in Teacher Education" (Paper presented at the Annual Meeting of the American Educational Research Association, New Orleans, 1984).
9. Judith Warren Little, "Teachers as Colleagues," in Virginia R. Koehler, (ed.), *The Educator's Handbook: Research into Practice* (New York: Longman, Inc., in press).
10. Beverly Showers, "Coaching: A Training Component for Facilitating Transfer of Training" (Paper presented at the Annual Meeting of the American Educational Research Association, Montreal, 1983).
11. Barnes and Edwards, *Effective Student Teaching.*
12. Susan S. Klein, "Student Influence on Teacher Behavior," *American Educational Research Journal* 8 (1971): 403–421; Thomas M. Sherman and William H. Cormier, "An Investigation of the Influence of Student Behavior on Teacher Behavior," *Journal of Applied Behavioral Analysis* 7 (1974): 11–21.
13. Frances F. Fuller and Oliver H. Bown, "Concerns of Teachers: A Developmental Conceptualization," *American Educational Research Journal* 6, no. 2 (1969): 207–226.
14. M. M. Cohn and V. Gellman, "Supervision: A Developmental Approach for Fostering Inquiry in Preservice Teacher Education" (Paper presented at the Annual Meeting of the American Educational Research Association, Chicago, 1985); Willis D. Copeland, "Student Teachers' Preference for Supervisory Approach, *Journal of Teacher Education* 33, no. 2 (1982): 32–36; D. Price and N. Sellars, "A Synthesis of Effective Teacher Behaviors in the Final Year of the Primary Practicum" (Paper presented at the Annual Meeting of the American Educational Research Association, Chicago, 1985).
15. Barnes and Edwards, *Effective Student Teaching*, p. 22.
16. See Kenneth M. Zeichner, "Alternative Paradigms of Teacher Education," *Journal of Teacher Education* 34, no. 3 (1983): 3–9.
17. Selected contributions to this line of inquiry include Jere E. Brophy and Carolyn M. Evertson, *Learning from Teaching* (Boston: Allyn and Bacon, 1976); John Elliot, "Developing Hypotheses about Classrooms from Teachers' Practical Constructs: An Account of the Work of the Ford Teaching Project," *Interchange* 7, no. 2 (1976–1977): 2–22; Rory O'Day, "Reality Teaching: The Self-Analysis Classroom," *Interchange* 5, no. 1 (1974): 36–45; W. J. Smyth, "Teachers as Collaborators in Clinical Supervision: Cooperative Learning about Teaching," *Teacher Education* 24 (1984): 60–68.
18. Smyth, "Teachers as Collaborators," p. 63.
19. Alan R. Tom, "Inquiring into Inquiry Teacher Education" (Paper presented at the Annual Meeting of the American Educational Research Association, Chicago, 1985).
20. Alan R. Tom offers Donald R. Cruickshank and Jane H. Applegate, "Reflective Teaching as a Strategy for Teacher Growth," *Educational Leadership* 38, no. 7 (1981): 553–54, as an example of teacher educators who would hold objectives constant while holding strategies problematic, and Kenneth M. Zeichner, "Reflective Teaching and Field-based Experience in Teacher Education," *Interchange* 12, no. 4 (1981–1982), as an example of a teacher educator who would hold both problematic.
21. Jean I. Erdman, "Assessing the Purposes of Early Field Experience Programs," *Journal of Teacher Education* 34, no. 4 (1983): 27–33.
22. For example, see John I. Goodlad, *A Place Called School* (New York: McGraw-Hill, 1983).
23. Barnes and Edwards, *Effective Student Teaching.*
24. The most prominent representatives of this literature include Morris L. Cogan, *Clinical Supervision* (Boston: Houghton Mifflin, 1973), and Keith Goldhammer, *Clinical Supervision: Special Methods for the Supervision of Teachers* (New York: Holt, Rinehart and Winston, 1969).
25. Barnes and Edwards, *Effective Student Teaching.*
26. Cohn and Gellman, "Supervision."
27. Copeland, "Cooperating Teacher Behavior and Student Teacher Classroom Performance"; Price and Sellars, "Effective Teacher Behaviors in the Primary Practicum."
28. Eliot Friedson, *Professional Dominance* (New York: Atherton Press, 1970).

29. Dan C. Lortie, *School Teacher: A Sociological Study* (Chicago: University of Chicago Press, 1975).
30. Susan J. Rosenholtz and S. J. Kyle, "Teacher Isolation: Barrier to Professionalism," *American Educator*, Winter 1984: 10–15.
31. Willis D. Copeland and J. R. Jamgochian, "Colleague Training and Peer Review," *Journal of Teacher Education* 36, no.2 (1985): 18–21.
32. F. A. J. Korthagen, "Reflective Thinking as a Basis for Teacher Education" (Paper presented at the Annual Meeting of the American Educational Research Association, Chicago, 1985).
33. F. A. J. Korthagen, "Reflective Thinking."

NOTES TO CHAPTER 3

1. Herbert Kohl, *On Teaching* (New York: Schocken Books, 1979), p. 11.
2. See, for example, Fred McDonald, "The Problems of Beginning Teachers: A Crisis in Training (Volume 1)," in *Study of induction programs for beginning teachers* (Princeton, NJ: Educational Testing Service, 1980); Sharon Feiman-Nemser, "Learning to Teach," in Lee S. Shulman and Gary Sykes, eds., *Handbook of Teaching and Policy* (New York: Longman, Inc., 1983).
3. *Beginning Teachers and Internship Programs*, Report No. 78–0014 (Washington, DC: National Institute of Education, 1979), p. 3.
4. For discussion of first-year teachers' responsibilities, see, for example, Judith Warren Little, "Teachers as Colleagues," in Virginia R. Koehler, ed., *The Educator's Handbook: Research into Practice*, (New York: Longman, Inc., in press); Sharon Feiman-Nemser, "Learning to Teach"; Carl A. Grant and Kenneth M. Zeichner, "Inservice Support for First-Year Teachers: The State of the Scene," *Journal of Research and Development in Education* 14 (1981): 99–111.
5. McDonald, "The Problems of Beginning Teachers."
6. Feiman-Nemser, "Learning to Teach."
7. James V. Hoffman and Maria E. Defino, "State and School District Intentions and the Implementation of New Teacher Programs" (Paper presented at the Annual Meeting of the American Educational Research Association, Chicago, IL, 1985).
8. Joseph Schwab, *Science, Curriculum, and Liberal Education*, eds. Ian Westbury and N. J. Wilof (Chicago: University of Chicago Press, 1978).
9. Simon Veenman, "Perceived Problems of Beginning Teachers," *Review of Educational Research* 54 (1984): 143–178.
10. Susan R. Sacks and Patricia Brady, "Who Teaches the City's Children? A Study of New York City's First-Year Teachers" (Paper presented at the Annual Meeting of the American Educational Research Association, Chicago, IL, 1985).
11. Feiman-Nemser, "Learning to Teach."
12. Gary A. Griffin and Hobart Hukill, "Teacher Induction Issues: Themes and Variation," in Gary A. Griffin and Hobart Hukill, eds., *First Years of Teaching: What Are the Pertinent Issues?* Report No. 9051 (Austin: The University of Texas at Austin, Research and Development Center for Teacher Education, 1983).
13. Feiman-Nemser, "Learning to Teach."
14. Paul Burden, "Teachers' Perceptions of Their Personal and Professional Development" (Paper presented at the Annual Meeting of the Midwestern Educational Research Association, Des Moines, 1981), p. 7.
15. McDonald, "The Problems of Beginning Teachers."
16. Feiman-Nemser, "Learning to Teach." In her analysis of schools which foster learning to teach, Feiman-Nemser draws upon findings from the Rand Corporation study of effective inservice programs reported in Milbrey McLaughlin and David Marsh, "Staff Development

and School Change," in Ann Lieberman and Lynne Miller, eds., *Staff Development: New Developments, New Realities, New Perspectives* (New York: Teachers College Press, 1979); and the study of effective staff development reported in Judith Warren Little, *School Success and Staff Development: The Role of Staff Development in Urban Desegregated Schools* (Boulder, CO: Center for Action Research, Inc., 1981).

17. Little, "Teachers as Colleagues."

18. Themes that emerged from conference discussion groups are reported in Griffin and Hukill, "Teacher Induction Issues: Themes and Variations."

19. Griffin and Hukill, "Teacher Induction Issues."

20. Griffin and Hukill, "Teacher Induction Issues."

21. Induction programs in which a single primary support person is identified are described in Leslie Huling-Austin, Susan Barnes, and John Smith, "A Research-based Development Program for Beginning Teachers" (Paper presented at the Annual Meeting of the American Educational Research Association, Chicago, 1985); Hoffman and Defino, "State and School District Intentions and the Implementation of New Teacher Programs"; and Sacks and Brady, "Who Teaches the City's Children?"

22. Janet M. Newberry, "The First Year of Experience: Influences on Beginning Teachers" (Paper presented at the annual meeting of the American Educational Research Association, New York, 1977).

23. Huling-Austin, Barnes, and Smith, "A Research-based Development Program for Beginning Teachers."

24. Phillip C. Schlechty and Deane Crowell, *Staff Development and School Improvement: A School District Examines Its Potential for Excellence*, Contract No. 400–79–0056 (Washington, DC: National Institute of Education, 1985).

25. Sacks and Brady, "Who Teaches the City's Children?"

26. Huling-Austin, Barnes, and Smith, "A Research-based Development Program for Beginning Teachers."

27. Sacks and Brady, "Who Teaches the City's Children?"

28. In "Perceived Problems of Beginning Teachers," Simon Veenman presents a list of 24 issues most often perceived as problems by beginning teachers. He compiled this list by selecting the 15 most serious problems in each of 83 empirical research studies — predominantly questionnaire studies. The 11 problems listed here were mentioned among the 15 most serious problems in at least 20% of the studies.

29. Hilda Borko and Rosary Lalik, "Learning to Teach: Beginning Teachers' Organization, Implementation and Evaluation of Reading Language Arts Instruction" (Paper presented at the Annual Meeting of the National Reading Conference, San Diego, 1985).

30. Gillian C. Cook, "Teachers Helping Teachers: A Training Program in Peer Supervision" (Paper presented at the Annual Conference of the Association of Teacher Educators, Las Vegas, 1986), p. 3.

31. D. A. Meyers, A. Michael, J. Langan, and C. Ashbaugh, "The Beginning Teacher Project: An Innovative School–University Program that Works" (Paper presented at the Annual Meeting of the American Association of Colleges of Teacher Education, Denver, 1985).

32. Huling-Austin, Barnes, and Smith, "A Research-based Development Program for Beginning Teachers."

33. Huling-Austin, Barnes, and Smith, "A Research-based Development Program for Beginning Teachers."

34. Laura A. Wagner, "The California Mentor Teacher Program: A Staff Development Initiative with Career Ladder Implications," unpublished manuscript.

35. Cook, "Teachers Helping Teachers."

36. Sara A. Edwards, *Changing Teacher Practice: A Synthesis of Relevant Research*, Report No. 9008 (Austin, TX: The University of Texas at Austin, Research and Development Center for Teacher Education, 1981).

NOTES TO CHAPTER 4

1. Chapters 2 and 3 in this book provide information regarding the skills teachers are expected to have at the end of preservice education and the induction period of teaching.
2. Arthur E. Wise, Linda Darling-Hammond, Milbrey W. McLaughlin, and Harriet T. Bernstein, *Teacher Evaluation: A Study of Effective Practice*, National Institute of Education Report R-3139-NIE (Santa Monica, CA: Rand, 1984).
3. The student descriptions of the ideal teacher are taken from interviews conducted as part of the Secondary School Recognition Program of the U.S. Secretary of Education. Students were asked to describe the teacher whom they most admired and respected. For further information see Beatrice A. Ward, *Features of Excellent Schools* (San Francisco: Center for Interactive Research and Development, 1985).
4. Professional teacher participation in collaborative research studies of teaching increased markedly during the past decade. For a sample of the impact of such participation on professional teacher development, see the following articles and reports: Gary A. Griffin, *Interactive Research and Development on Schooling: Antecedents, Purposes, and Significance for School Improvement* (Austin, TX: The University of Texas at Austin, Research and Development Center for Teacher Education, 1983); Sharon N. Oja and Gerald J. Pine, *A Two-Year Study of Teachers' Stages of Development in Relation to Collaborative Action Research in Schools* (Durham, NH: University of New Hampshire, 1983); Leslie L. Huling, "The Effects on Teachers of Participation in a Collaborative Action Research Program" (Paper presented at the Annual Meeting of the American Educational Research Association, New York, 1983); and William J. Tikunoff, Beatrice A. Ward, and Gary A. Griffin, *Interactive Research and Development on Teaching: Final Report* (San Francisco, CA: Far West Laboratory for Educational Research and Development, 1979).
5. In October, 1984, the Research and Development Center for Teacher Education at The University of Texas at Austin sponsored a conference on the state of the art in teacher education. Two chapters in the report of this conference provide up-to-date information regarding the state of professional teacher development: Kenneth R. Howey, "Six Major Functions of Staff Development: A Selective Review of the Literature," and Beatrice A. Ward, "Teacher Development: The Challenge of the Future," in Shirley M. Hord, Sharon F. O'Neal, and Martha L. Smith, eds., *Beyond the Looking Glass* (Austin, TX: The University of Texas at Austin, Research and Development Center for Teacher Education, 1985).
6. Gary A. Griffin, Susan Barnes, Sharon O'Neal, Sara A. Edwards, Maria E. Defino, and Hobart Hukill, *Changing Teacher Practice: Final Report of an Experimental Study*, Report No. 9052 (Austin, TX: The University of Texas at Austin, Research and Development Center for Teacher Education, 1984); and Kenneth R. Howey and Joseph C. Vaughan, "Current Patterns of Staff Development," in Gary A. Griffin, ed., *Staff Development*, Eighty-second Yearbook of the Society for the Study of Education (Chicago, IL: University of Chicago Press, 1983), 92-117.
7. Phillip C. Schlechty, Deane Crowell, Betty L. Whitford, and Anne W. Joslin, *Understanding and Managing Staff Development in an Urban School System: Executive Summary* (Chapel Hill, NC: University of North Carolina, 1984).
8. Ward, "Teacher Development."
9. M. Levine, *Excellence in Education: Some Lessons from America's Best Run Companies and Schools* (Washington, DC: American Enterprise Institute, 1984).
10. Howey and Vaughan, *Current Patterns of Staff Development*.
11. Susan J. Rosenholtz, *Political Myths About Reforming the Teaching Profession*, Working Paper No. 4 (Denver, CO: Education Commission of the States, 1984).
12. Ward, "Teacher Development."
13. Stuart C. Purkey and Marshall S. Smith, "Effective Schools: A Review," *The Elementary School Journal* 83, no. 4 (March 1983): 427-452.

14. According to the RITE framework, participation of an entire faculty in a clinical teacher education program depends upon the purposes of the training that is to take place. If a program were part of a total school improvement effort, all teachers and administrators in a school would be involved. However, the framework can apply to training for a smaller group of teachers whose growth and development requires acquisition of a particular set of skills or increased knowledge regarding a subject matter area, the learning needs of students at a particular age, and so forth.

15. For example see Rosenholtz, *Political Myths*, and Judith Warren Little, "School Success and Staff Development in Urban Desegregated Schools: A Summary of Recently Completed Research" (Paper presented at the Annual Meeting of the American Educational Research Association, Los Angeles, 1981).

16. Ward, "Teacher Development"; Howey, "Six Major Functions"; and Purkey and Smith, "Effective Schools."

17. The participatory/collaborative feature of the RITE framework builds on the collaborative approaches to educational research and development that have been studied during the past ten years. The importance of working *with* rather than *on* teachers was pointed out some ten years ago in the original study of interactive research and development. See Tikunoff, Ward, and Griffin, *Interactive Research and Development on Teaching*

18. Oja and Pine, *A Two-Year Study of Teachers' Stages of Development*, and Grant Behnke, "Report from the Field: An IR&D Participant Comments," *R&DCTE Review* 1, no. 3 (September 1983): 3.

19. Process-product research on teaching is discussed in numerous papers, articles, and books. Examples of the findings from this research can be found in Charles W. Fisher, David C. Berliner, Nikola N. Filby, Richard Marliave, Leonard S. Cahen, and Marilyn M. Dishaw, "Teaching Behaviors, Academic Learning Time, and Student Achievement: An Overview," in Carolyn H. Denham and Ann Lieberman, eds., *Time to Learn* (Washington, DC: National Institute of Education, 1980); and Barak Rosenshine, "Teaching Functions in Instructional Programs," *The Elementary School Journal* 84, no. 4 (March 1983): 335-352.

20. Chapter 1 of this book provides a more extensive discussion of the knowledge bases the RITE framework attends.

21. For examples see Ward, "Teacher Development," and Richard C. Wallace, Jr., "The Schenley High School Teacher Center," in Shirley M. Hord, Sharon F. O'Neal, and Martha L. Smith, eds., *Beyond the Looking Glass* (Austin, TX: The University of Texas at Austin, Research and Development Center for Teacher Education, 1985).

22. Bruce Joyce and Beverly Showers, "Transfer of Training: The Contribution of 'Coaching,'" *Journal of Education* 163, no. 2 (Spring 1981): 163-172.

23. Howey and Vaughan, "Current Patterns of Staff Development," and Ward, "Teacher Development."

24. Schlechty et al., *Understanding and Managing Staff Development*.

25. Griffin et al., *Changing Teacher Practice*.

26. Levine, *Excellence in Education*.

27. Norman A. Sprinthall and Lois Thies-Sprinthall, "The Teacher as an Adult Learner: A Cognitive-Developmental View," in Gary A. Griffin, ed., *Staff Development*, Eighty-second Yearbook of the Society for the Study of Education (Chicago, IL: University of Chicago Press, 1983), 13-35.

28. Schlechty et al., *Understanding and Managing Staff Development*.

29. Originally proposed in Ward, "Teacher Development."

30. Howey, "Six Major Functions of Staff Development."

31. Gary A. Griffin, *The School As a Workplace and the Master Teacher Concept*, Report No. 9053 (Austin, TX: The University of Texas at Austin, Research and Development Center for Teacher Education, 1984), and John I. Goodlad, *A Place Called School: Prospects for the Future* (New York: McGraw-Hill Book Company, 1983).

32. As recently as 1983, authors in the National Society for the Study of Education Yearbook on staff development did not mention a staged career for teachers as part of a comprehensive set of reviews and recommendations regarding inservice teacher education. Much of the current attention to this matter has been generated since the report from the National Commission on Excellence in Education, *A Nation at Risk: The Imperative for Educational Reform* (Washington, DC: U. S. Government Printing Office, 1983), which called for recognition of teacher excellence, as did other reports, such as the one from the Education Commission of the States, *Action for Excellence: A Comprehensive Plan to Improve our Nation's Schools* (Denver, CO: Education Commission of the States, 1983), that were released after the NSSE Yearbook was published.

33. For examples see Howey and Vaughan, "Current Patterns of Staff Development"; Ward, "Teacher Development"; Wise, Darling-Hammond, McLaughlin, and Bernstein, *Teacher Evaluation;* and Wallace, "The Schenley High School Teacher Center."

34. The Charlotte-Mecklenburg Career Development Program has received considerable attention as a model approach to professional teacher development based on a staged career. For a discussion of the program, see Phillip C. Schlechty, "A Framework for Evaluating Induction into Teaching," in Shirley M. Hord, Sharon F. O'Neal, and Martha L. Smith, eds., *Beyond the Looking Glass* (Austin, TX: The University of Texas at Austin, Research and Development Center for Teacher Education, 1985).

35. Griffin, *The School As a Workplace,* and Rosenholtz, *Political Myths.*

36. Sprinthall and Thies-Sprinthall, "The Teacher as an Adult Learner."

37. Rosenholtz, *Political Myths;* Patricia T. Ashton, "Teacher Efficacy: A Motivational Paradigm for Effective Teacher Education," *Journal of Teacher Education* 35, no. 5 (September–October 1984): 28–32; and Judith Warren Little, "Norms of Collegiality and Experimentation: Workplace Conditions of School Success," *American Educational Research Journal* 19, no. 3 (1982): 325–340. Also see Griffin's discussion in Chapter 1.

38. Griffin et al., *Changing Teacher Practice.*

NOTES TO CHAPTER 5

1. Ann Lieberman and Lynne Miller, *Teachers, Their World and Their Work* (Washington, DC: Association for Supervision and Curriculum Development, 1984); Seymour Sarason, *The Culture of the School and the Problem of Change* (Boston: Allyn & Bacon, 1982); John I. Goodlad, "The School as a Workplace," in Gary A. Griffin, ed., *Staff Development* (Chicago: University of Chicago Press, 1983); Sharon Feiman-Nemser, "Learning to Teach," in Lee S. Shulman and Gary Sykes, eds., *Handbook of Teaching and Policy* (New York: Longman, 1983).

2. Judith E. Lanier, "Research on Teacher Education," in *Handbook of Research on Teaching,* 3rd ed. (New York: Macmillan, in press), p. 53.

3. Arthur E. Wise, *Legislated Learning: The Bureaucratization of the American Classroom* (Berkeley: University of California Press, 1979); Michael Apple, "Curricular Form and the Logic of Technical Control," in Michael Apple and Lois Weis, eds., *Ideology and Practice in Education* (Philadelphia: Temple University Press, 1983); Gary Sykes, "Contradictions, Ironies, and Promises Unfulfilled: A Contemporary Account of the Status of Teaching," *Phi Delta Kappan* 65, no. 2 (1983): 87–93.

4. Kenneth M. Zeichner, "Individual and Institutional Influences on the Development of Teacher Perspectives," in Lillian Katz and James Raths, eds., *Advances in Teacher Education,* Volume II (Norwood, NJ: Ablex, in press).

5. Michael Fullan and Alan Pomfret, "Research on Curriculum and Instruction Implementation," *Review of Educational Research* 47 (Spring 1977): 335–397.

6. Gary A. Griffin, "Implications of Research for Staff Development Programs," *Elementary School Journal* 83 (November 1983): 414–425.

7. Fullan and Pomfret, "Research on Curriculum and Instruction Implementation," p. 337. Also see Neal Gross, Joseph Giacquinta, and Marilyn Bernstein, *Implementing Organizational Innovations: A Sociological Analysis of Planned Educational Change* (New York: Basic Books, 1971).

8. Peter Burger and Thomas Luchmann, *The Social Construction of Reality* (New York: Doubleday, 1967), p. 55.

9. See Sarason, *The Culture of the School and the Problem of Change,* for discussion of this issue in relation to schools in particular.

10. Thomas Popkewitz, "Change and Stability in Schooling: The Dual Quality of Educational Reform (Geelong, Australia: Deakin University Press, 1983), p. 9.

11. See Donald Light, Jr., "Surface and Deep Structure: Observing the Organization of Professional Training," *Administrative Science Quarterly* 24 (December 1979): 552–569, for a discussion of these different layers of institutional reality.

12. Thomas Popkewitz, "Educational Reform and the Problem of Institutional Life," *Educational Researcher* 8, no. 3 (1979): 3–8; John I. Goodlad, M. Frances Klein and Associates, *Looking Behind the Classroom Door* (Worthington, OH: Charles A. Jones, 1970); Sarason, *The Culture of the School and the Problem of Change.*

13. Fullan and Pomfret, "Research on Curriculum and Instruction Implementation," p. 345.

14. Malcolm Parlett and David Hamilton, "Evaluation as Illumination: A New Approach to the Study of Innovatory Programs," in Gene Glass, ed., *Evaluation Studies Review Annual,* Volume I (Beverly Hills, CA: Sage, 1976).

15. Thomas Popkewitz, B. Robert Tabachnick, and Gary Wehlage, *The Myth of Educational Reform* (Madison: The University of Wisconsin Press, 1982); Popkewitz, "Educational Reform and the Problem of Institutional Life"; Sarason, *The Culture of the School and the Problem of Change.*

16. The findings from this evaluation study are summarized in two publications: Popkewitz, Tabachnick, and Wehlage, *The Myth of Educational Reform,* and Thomas Romberg, ed., *Toward Effective Schooling: The IGE Experience* (Lanham, MD: University Press of America, 1985).

17. See Popkewitz, Tabachnick, and Wehlage, *The Myth of Educational Reform,* pp. 22–40; Romberg, *Toward Effective Schooling,* pp. 19–38.

18. Romberg, *Toward Effective Schooling.* Thomas Romberg and Gary Price, in their chapter on "Curriculum Change as Cultural Change," in Gary A. Griffin, ed., *Staff Development* (Chicago: University of Chicago Press, 1983), pp. 167–170, discuss the differences between nominal change, which involves changes in nothing but labels, and three types of actual change: technical change, illusory change, and constructive change.

19. Popkewitz, Tabachnick, and Wehlage, *The Myth of Educational Reform,* p. 4.

20. See Popkewitz, Tabachnick, and Wehlage, *The Myth of Educational Reform,* pp. 61–160, for descriptions of the implementation of IGE in technical, illusory, and constructive schools.

21. Romberg, *Toward Effective Schooling,* p. 220.

22. Popkewitz, Tabachnick, and Wehlage, *The Myth of Educational Reform,* p. 173.

23. See B. Othanel Smith, *A Design for a School of Pedagogy* (Washington, DC: U.S. Department of Education, 1980), and Bruce Joyce and Renee Clift, "The Phoenix Agenda: Essential Reform in Teacher Education," *Educational Researcher* 13, no. 4 (1984): 5–18, for discussion of some of the most significant reform proposals directed at preservice teacher education.

24. See John I. Goodlad, "The Reconstruction of Teacher Education, *Teachers College Record* 72 (September 1970), 61–72; Smith, *A Design for a School of Pedagogy;* and Kenneth R. Howey, Sam A. Yarger, and Bruce Joyce, *Improving Teacher Education* (Washington, DC: Association of Teacher Educators, 1978). Also see W. John Smyth, "Developing a Critical Practice of Clinical Supervision," *Journal of Curriculum Studies* 17, no. 1 (1985): 1–15, for a discussion of how clinical supervision has been implemented in a manner inconsistent with the intentions of the original designers of the approach.

25. Goodlad, "The Reconstruction of Teacher Education."
26. David Clark and Gerald Marker, "The Institutionalization of Teacher Education," in Kevin Ryan, ed., *Teacher Education* (Chicago: University of Chicago Press, 1975), p. 52.
27. Fullan and Pomfret, "Research on Curriculum and Instruction Implementation," pp. 361-365.
28. Fullan and Pomfret, "Research on Curriculum and Instruction Implementation," pp. 367-390.
29. The following discussion will focus on the characteristics of preservice and inservice teacher education and will include induction in the discussion of inservice characteristics because of the lack of attention to induction on a wide scale until recently.
30. Phillip C. Schlechty, Julius George, and Betty Lou Whitford, "Reform in Teacher Education and the Professionalization of Teaching," *High School Journal* 61 (April 1978): 313-320; Clark and Marker, "The Institutionalization of Teacher Education."
31. Joyce and Clift, "The Phoenix Agenda."
32. Martin Haberman, "Research on Preservice Laboratory and Clinical Experiences," in Kenneth R. Howey and William Gardner, eds., *The Education of Teachers: A Look Ahead* (New York: Longman, 1983).
33. Donald Moore and Arthur Hyde, *Making Sense of Staff Development: An Analysis of Staff Development Programs and Their Costs in Three Urban School Districts* (Chicago: Designs for Change, 1981).
34. Phillip C. Schlechty and D. Crowell, *Understanding and Managing Staff Development in an Urban School System* (Chapel Hill: University of North Carolina, 1983), p. 49.
35. Lanier, "Research on Teacher Education," p. 123.
36. Kenneth R. Howey and Joseph C. Vaughan, "Current Patterns of Staff Development," in Gary A. Griffin, ed., *Staff Development* (Chicago: University of Chicago Press, 1983).
37. Carl A. Grant and Kenneth M. Zeichner, "Inservice Support for First Year Teachers: The State of the Scene," *Journal of Research and Development in Education* 14, no. 2 (1981): 99-111.
38. Bruce Peseau and Paul Orr, *An Academic and Financial Study of Teacher Education Programs Through the Doctoral Level in Public State Universities and Land Grant Colleges* (Montgomery: University of Alabama, 1979); Bruce Peseau and Paul Orr, "The Outrageous Underfunding of Teacher Education," *Phi Delta Kappan* 62, no. 2 (1980): 100-102; Bruce Peseau and Paul Orr, *The Second Annual Academic and Financial Study of Teacher Education Programs in Senior State Universities and Land Grant Colleges, 1978-79* (Montgomery: University of Alabama, 1981).
39. Bruce Peseau, "Developing an Adequate Resource Base for Teacher Education," *Journal of Teacher Education* 33, no. 4 (1982): 14.
40. John Palmer, "Teacher Education: A Perspective from a Major Public University," in Charles Case and William Matthes, eds., *Colleges of Education: Perspectives on Their Future* (Berkeley: McCutchan, 1985).
41. See Lanier, "Research on Teacher Education," for a discussion of these underlying causes.
42. Howey and Vaughan, "Current Patterns of Staff Development," p. 96.
43. Moore and Hyde, "Making Sense of Staff Development."
44. Bruce Joyce, Kenneth R. Howey, and Sam A. Yarger, *ISTE Report I: Issues to Face* (Syracuse, NY: Syracuse University, National Dissemination Center, 1977).
45. Joyce, Howey, and Yarger, *ISTE Report I.*
46. Clark and Marker, "The Institutionalization of Teacher Education."
47. Lanier, "Research on Teacher Education," p. 104.
48. Harry Judge, *American Graduate Schools of Education: A View from Abroad* (New York: Ford Foundation, 1982).
49. Kenneth M. Zeichner and Daniel Liston, "Theory and Practice in the Evolution of an Inquiry-Oriented Student Teaching Program" (Paper presented at the Annual Meeting of the American Educational Research Association, Chicago, 1985).

50. Lanier, "Research on Teacher Education," p. 8.
51. Clark and Marker, "The Institutionalization of Teacher Education."
52. Moore and Hyde, "Making Sense of Staff Development," p. 105.
53. Harry Hutson, "Inservice Best Practices: The Learnings of General Education," *Journal of Research and Development in Education* 14, no. 2 (1981): 1–10.
54. Dan C. Lortie, *Schoolteacher: A Sociological Study* (Chicago: University of Chicago Press, 1975).
55. Bruce Joyce, "The Ecology of Professional Development," in Eric Hoyle and Jacquetta Megarry, eds., *World Yearbook of Education 1980: Professional Development of Teachers* (London: Nichols, 1980).
56. Lanier, "Research on Teacher Education," p. 108.
57. Clark and Marker, "The Institutionalization of Teacher Education."
58. Clark and Marker, "The Institutionalization of Teacher Education."
59. Lanier, "Research on Teacher Education," p. 78.
60. Zeichner and Liston, "Theory and Practice in the Evolution of an Inquiry-Oriented Student Teaching Program."
61. Phillip C. Schlechty and Betty Lou Whitford, "The Organizational Context of School Systems and the Functions of Staff Development," in Gary A. Griffin, ed., *Staff Development* (Chicago: University of Chicago Press, 1983); Judith Warren Little, "Seductive Images and Organizational Realities in Professional Development," *Teachers College Record* 86, no. 1 (1984): 84–102.
62. Joyce, "The Ecology of Professional Development," p. 28.
63. Kenneth R. Howey, "Teacher Education: An Overview," in Kenneth R. Howey and William Gardner, eds., *Teacher Education: A Look Ahead* (New York: Longman, 1983), based on a survey reported in Bruce Joyce, Sam A. Yarger, and Kenneth R. Howey, *Preservice Teacher Education* (Palo Alto, CA: Booksend Laboratory, 1977).
64. David Clark and Egon Guba, *A Study of Teacher Education Institutions as Innovators* (Bloomington: Indiana University, 1976); Joyce and Clift, "The Phoenix Agenda."
65. Gary D. Fenstermacher and David C. Berliner, "Determining the Value of Staff Development," *Elementary School Journal* 85, no. 3 (1985): 281–314; Gary A. Griffin, "The Work of Staff Development," in Gary A. Griffin, ed., *Staff Development* (Chicago: University of Chicago Press, 1983).
66. Frederick R. Cyphert and Ernest Spaights, *An Analysis and Projection of Research on Teacher Education*, Cooperative Research Project No. F-15 (Columbus: Ohio State University, 1964), p. 114.
67. Joyce and Clift, "The Phoenix Agenda."
68. Lanier, "Research on Teacher Education"; Feiman-Nemser, "Learning to Teach"; John McIntyre, *Field Experience in Teacher Education* (Washington, DC: Foundation for Excellence in Teacher Education and the ERIC Clearinghouse on Teacher Education, 1983); Kenneth M. Zeichner, "Myths and Realities: Field-Based Experiences in Preservice Teacher Education," *Journal of Teacher Education* 31, no. 6 (1980): 45–55.
69. Kenneth M. Zeichner, "Content and Contexts: Neglected Elements in Studies of Student Teaching as an Occasion for Learning to Teach," *Journal of Education for Teaching*, in press.
70. Moore and Hyde, "Making Sense of Staff Development."
71. Little, "Seductive Images and Organizational Realities in Professional Development."
72. Lieberman and Miller, "Teachers, Their World and Their Work"; Sara Freedman, Jane Jackson, and Katherine Boles, "Teaching: An Imperiled Profession," in Lee S. Shulman and Gary Sykes, eds., *Handbook of Teaching and Policy* (New York: Longman, 1983).
73. Brian Crittenden, "Some Prior Questions in the Reform of Teacher Education," *Interchange* 4, nos. 2–3 (1973): 1–12.
74. See Kenneth M. Zeichner, "Alternative Paradigms of Teacher Education," *Journal of Teacher Education* 34, no. 3 (1983): 3–9; and Anthony Harnett and Michael Naish, "Techni-

cians or Social Bandits? Some Moral and Political Issues in the Education of Teachers," in Peter Woods, ed., *Teacher Strategies: Explorations in Sociology of the School* (Driffield, England: Nafferton Books, 1980). Also, there may be agreement over the degree to which a teacher education program should reflect present practices in schools, but not the degree to which the social, economic, and political policies that affect the conduct of schooling should be accepted as given. See Crittenden, "Some Prior Questions in the Reform of Teacher Education," for discussion of this issue.

75. See James Lynch and H. Dudley Plunkett, *Teacher Education and Cultural Change* (London: George Allen and Unwin, 1973), for discussion of the relationship between the preconceptions underlying education in a society and expectations for teacher roles in teacher education programs.

76. See Merle Borrowman, *The Liberal and Technical in Teacher Education* (New York: Teachers College Press, 1956); and Kenneth M. Zeichner, "Preparation for Elementary Teaching," in Peter Burke and Robert Heideman, eds., *Career-Long Teacher Education* (Springfield, IL: Charles Thomas, 1985), for further discussion of this distinction. Also see Judith E. Lanier, *The Future of Teacher Education: Two Papers*, Occasional Paper No. 79 (East Lansing, MI: Institute for Research on Teaching, 1984) for an analogous discussion of differences in expectations for the teacher's role.

77. Lanier, *The Future of Teacher Education*, p. 6.

78. See Zeichner, "Content and Contexts: Neglected Elements in Studies of Student Teaching as an Occasion for Learning to Teach," for discussion of two different positions on the source and substance of this knowledge base.

79. Much of the literature advocates an even more limited role for the teacher than that of skilled craftsperson: the teacher as technician. See Gary Sykes, "Contradictions, Ironies, and Promises Unfulfilled"; Michael Apple, "Curricular Form and the Logic of Technical Control"; and Kenneth M. Zeichner, "The Deskilling of Teachers and the Phenomenon of Teacher Stress," *Teacher Education* (in press) for further discussion and documentation of this point.

80. Max Van Mannen, "Linking Ways of Knowing with Ways of Being Practical," *Curriculum Inquiry* 6, no. 3 (1977): 205–228. See Kenneth M. Zeichner and Dan Liston, "Varieties of Discourse in Supervisory Conferences," *Teaching and Teacher Education* 1, no. 2 (1985): 155–174, and Kenneth M. Zeichner and Kenneth Teitelbaum, "Personalized and Inquiry-Oriented Teacher Education," *Journal of Education for Teaching* 9, no. 2 (1982): 95–117, for discussion of Van Mannen's work in relation to the clinical education of teachers.

81. Maxine Greene, "The Matter of Mystification: Teacher Education in Unquiet Times," in *Landscapes of Learning* (New York: Teachers College Press, 1979); Kenneth M. Zeichner, "Reflective Teaching and Field-Based Experience in Teacher Education," *Interchange* 12, no. 4 (1981): 1–22.

82. Gary D. Fenstermacher, "On Learning to Teach Effectively from Research on Teacher Effectiveness," in Carolyn Denham and Ann Lieberman, eds., *Time to Learn* (Washington, DC: National Institute of Education, 1980), p. 129.

83. Robert Floden, "The Role of Rhetoric in Changing Teachers' Beliefs," *Teaching and Teacher Education* 1, no. 1 (1985): 19–32; Karen Kepler Zumwalt, "Research on Teaching: Policy Implications for Teacher Education," in Milbrey W. McLaughlin and Ann Lieberman, eds., *Policy Making in Education* (Chicago: University of Chicago Press, 1982); Margaret Buchmann, "The Use of Research Knowledge in Teacher Education and Teaching," *American Journal of Education* 92 (August 1984): 421–439.

84. Fenstermacher, "On Learning to Teach Effectively."

85. Fullan and Pomfret, "Research on Curriculum and Instruction Implementation," pp. 367–390.

86. Romberg and Price, "Curriculum Implementation and Staff Development as Cultural Change."

87. Fullan and Pomfret, "Research on Curriculum and Instruction Implementation," pp. 368–371.

88. Joyce and Clift, "The Phoenix Agenda"; Clark and Marker, "The Institutionalization of Teacher Education"; Lanier, "Research on Teacher Education"; and John Palmer, "The Failure of Schools of Education," *The Texas Humanist* (Fall 1984).